WELCOME TO
CLUB MOM

THE ADVENTURE BEGINS

WELCOME TO
CLUB MOM

THE ADVENTURE BEGINS

Leslie Lehr Spirson

Illustrations by Jack Lindstrom

CompCare® Publishers

Minneapolis, Minnesota

Published in the United States by CompCare Publishers.
Reproduction in whole or part, in any form, including storage in
memory device system, is forbidden without written permission,
except that portions may be used in broadcast or printed
commentary or review when attributed fully to authors and
publication by names.

Library of Congress Cataloging-in-Publication Data
Spirson, Leslie Lehr.
    Welcome to Club Mom: the adventure begins / Leslie Lehr Spirson
    p.   cm.
    ISBN 0-89638-255-9
    1. Motherhood—Humor. 2. Mothers—Psychology—Humor.
3. Pregnancy—Humor. I. Title.
HQ759.S655   1991
306.874'3'0207—dc20   91-16099
                                                                    CIP

Illustrations by Jack Lindstrom
Cover and interior design by MacLean and Tuminelly

Inquiries, orders, and catalog requests should be addressed to:
CompCare Publishers
2415 Annapolis Lane
Minneapolis, Minnesota 55441
612/559-4800
Toll free 800/328-3330

   6   5   4   3   2   1
96 95 94 93 92 91

Contents

Welcome to Club Mom! 1

CLUB MOM INITIATION

One with the Universe 5

Pit Stops...9

How to Break the News 15

Scheduling Your Morning Sickness...............17

Cosmetic Camouflage 21

I Am Not YOUR Mother!.................................24

When in Doubt: Accessorize............................25

Battle of the Sexes...29

Things Your Doctor Never Told You 33

Sex Appeal..35

Erotic Massage 38

Baby Showers...41

Natural Childbirth Classes 45

What? Me, Worry? 47

HOSPITAL HANDBOOK

Just Say Yes..51

Queen for a Day...55

Visitors..58

Spitting Image 60

Not Just Another Pretty Chest 63
Sleep...67
Bonding..69
Going Solo...73

LIFETIME MEMBERSHIP GUARANTEED
Now What? 81
Best Bets for Bed 83
Whose Body Is It, Anyway? 85
Simplifying Your Beauty Routine......................................87
Don't Leave Home without It 88
You Are Not Alone..90
Pacifiers Are for Pacifying..93
Is There Sex After Childbirth? 96
Vital Questions...101
Crawling Can Be Hazardous to Your Health 103
Spoiling and the "N" Word...104
Twenty-Four-Hour Leave 107
The Six O'Clock Scramble 109

KISS IT GOOD-BYE
Old Friends 113
Satin Sheets 115
Night Owling 118
Privacy 121
Telephone Time 124
Night Life..127
Discussions of World Peace...129

HAZARDS FOR NEW MEMBERS

The Experts 133
Other Kids 135
Other Moms..136
Your Mother..139
Your Mother-in-Law 141
The Kitchen..143
Baby-Sitters 145
Birthday Parties 149
The Three R's 150
College Savings Plans...152
Playing Favorites 155

MEMBERSHIP MYTHS

Nap When the Baby Naps 161
All Babies Are Beautiful......................................162
Grandmas Bake Cookies 164
A Baby's Place Is in the Home................................165
Having It All 167
Quality Time 171
Children Should Be Seen and Not Heard 173
Traveling Light 175

CAREER WOMAN BLUES

They Used to Call Them Old Maids 183
R-E-S-P-E-C-T...186
But What Do You Do All Day?................................189
Ego, Ergo, I Go 192
Working at Home 193

PAST THE PLEDGE STAGE: PLANNING FOR NUMBER TWO

Once More—with Feeling 197

About the Author 201

This book is dedicated with love to Jon, for his tender husbanding, his passionate fathering, and his frequent diapering...to my precious daughter, Juliette, for providing joy and membership in The Club... her splendid Aunt Tracy, who I'm saving a seat for...and to my mother, Dr. Claire J. Lehr, for her professional and personal expertise—now I understand.

Also to Barbara for showing me the ropes, Cheryl and June for making Club meetings so much fun, Buckeye moms Dayna and Judi, local moms Kay and Wendy...and to mothers everywhere. ENJOY!

Welcome to Club Mom!

Welcome to Club Mom is a humorous guide to the real-life aspects of pregnancy and the first year of motherhood. It fills a gap between dozens of books on childbirth and dozens more on parenting. Its focus is not, however, on the child, but on Mom herself.

Welcome to Club Mom is for pregnant career women who have never seen the interior of a diaper and for new mothers who are still in a state of shock over the changes in their lives. It's a lively rap session with someone who's been there recently herself—Leslie Lehr Spirson.

Frank and funny as it is, *Welcome to Club Mom* is a stand-up cheer for motherhood as one of life's true joys. At the same time, the kind of friendly—even intimate—information offered here takes Club Mom beyond ordinary parent-humor books and closer to the how-to section.

You, the pregnant reader, will learn about "Scheduling Your Morning Sickness" and how to revel in "Sex Appeal." At the hospital, you'll be assured that it's all right to "Just Say Yes" to drugs (if you choose to) and to take advantage of your role as "Queen for a Day." If you're a single mother, you'll gain confidence in "Going Solo."

Once home with the baby, you, the new mother, will be comforted by the realization that "You Are Not Alone" and relieved at the answer to: "Is There Sex After Childbirth?" You will understand why you can kiss your "Old Friends" good-bye, along with your "Privacy."

You will be duly warned about "The Experts" and "College Savings Plans." Painlessly you will uncover myths like "Nap When the Baby Naps" and "Having It All." Your career-woman blues will be assuaged by a new kind of "R-E-S-P-E-C-T."

Welcome to Club Mom is a fresh, positive approach to the age-old practice of child-bearing. It is full of information that your doctor doesn't tell you and your mother has forgotten, that you won't otherwise know until you do it.

The author's mother, Claire J. Lehr, has a Ph.D. in child development. Leslie Lehr Spirson's lifelong exposure to this kind of expertise, along with her own recent experiences (her daughter, Juliette, has just reached her first birthday) and informal talks with other new mothers, led to the creation of *Welcome to Club Mom*.

CLUB MOM
INITIATION

One with the Universe

Have you ever been at a party where everyone else was engrossed in a conversation about someone or something you knew absolutely nothing about? You felt as if you'd changed worlds—or at least towns.

Well, you're going to feel that way for nine long months. And I don't mean just at parties. For the whole of your pregnancy, you will be on a completely alien plane of existence. Although you will continue to function as a normal human being, and outwardly SEEM like a normal human being, such normalcy is all a lie. Go ahead, feign interest in Budapest or Baghdad. Pretend you care about the plight of the American auto industry. No one will know that you're distracted by an all-consuming secret: YOU'RE PREGNANT.

Being pregnant, of course, is not much of a secret once your belly beats you through the doorway. Still, as you are rapidly learning, it is like being the only one in on a big cosmic joke. HA, HA.

First, your left brain organizational skills will falter—you will forget things. What's more, you will no longer care about those silly details that used to keep you up at night. Like forgetting to carry the "1" in your budget report. Don't tell your boss…you'll notice in time to fix it. Here's the best part: you won't even be upset about it!

Then your right brain, the creative side, will go. Don't worry, you won't lose it. It will just be diverted (like your energy) toward baby-centered projects—specifically, toward the nursery. I spent weeks pondering paint samples and months committing to crib sheets. I visited the furniture store weekly and changed my mind the day before the crib was due to be delivered. Never fear. This occupation with infant-oriented decor evaporates in the third trimester, once the baby is mostly developed. Then you just have to deal with the awkwardness of having a small soccer player inside you.

Now that you are in this blessed state of "waiting," everyone you normally come in contact with will be concerned about your physical well-being. That is, they are concerned generally with the broad picture of how you are. They don't really want to hear the gritty details. After all, do YOU really want to know about your great-uncle's prostate?

You'll find that other first-time-pregnant women are truly interested, not only to compare notes, but also to share the misery. If you are talking with women who have not yet experienced pregnancy, keep mum. Don't scare them off. To a person who is thoroughly embarrassed at the hushed mention of the word "hemorrhoid," there is no way to describe the joyous feelings in a way that justifies the physical discomforts.

The whole time I was pregnant, I was utterly occupied with trying to recognize each twinge and every stirring within. I was thrilled at the sudden urgency of my body to refuel. Within seconds of being a relatively undemanding individual, I would require immediate nourishment. To avoid these unmerciful attacks, I always carried snacks and I ate before dinner parties. Even so, my husband elbowed his way into more than one buffet line with a cry of "pregnant wife!" My body was definitely boss.

Now that it is over, however, I mostly remember how different I felt then from how I feel now. Different emotionally. Different because pregnancy seems to provide a strange psychic connection with the earth and the stars. When you raise your eyebrows at mothers who wish they were pregnant again, remember that this feeling is more than a maternal instinct. It is that singular indescribable feeling of DIFFERENCE.

Vive la différence!

God could not be everywhere and therefore he made mothers.

—*The Talmud*

Pit Stops

You'll never forget your first symptom of pregnancy. I know I won't. I was visiting my father, The Scientist. We were doing our usual father-daughter thing: going to as many movies as we can possibly fit into one day. We had already finished the catching-up-with-our-lives talk and were in line for popcorn. He was amazed that they actually offered "butter flavor," rather than the real thing.

I nonchalantly mentioned that there was a chance that I might be pregnant. An avid people watcher, my father generally just nodded at the appropriate intervals in my scintillating conversation. Not this time. His analytical antennae were up and he was listening. He turned to me immediately and asked, "Is that why you have to go to the bathroom so often?"

This was news to me. I had naturally assumed that since my bladder was the size of a pea, my trips to the powder room between films would guarantee that I didn't miss any major plot points. Besides, everyone knows from the movies that the first symptom of pregnancy is fainting. I know now that this is a grave misconception reinforced only for purposes of visual drama. Fainting doesn't start until later, when all the extra blood can be a strain on the system when you stand up quickly. At the time, I just stared at my father. Stunned at his radar reception, I shrugged off the question.

But, sure enough, I was pregnant. For nine months, I never went longer than two hours without a pit stop. According to the pregnancy manuals, if you are taking a road trip or even sitting at work, you should get up often and move around to help circulate all that blood. In truth, they are giving you a delicate excuse to get up and go pee. The problem is, you don't always have to go—you just feel like you do.

This will change your priorities in terms of redecorating. I told my husband, "Either that bathroom wallpaper is history, or I am!" I covered our beautiful but cold parquet hallway that leads to the bathroom with a carpet remnant. You will learn quickly that maternity jumpsuits are cute, but not very practical, especially when you leave the safe and comparatively sanitary facilities of your home for public cubicles. You will swear off liquids after 6:00 P.M. Late-night cocoa will join the list of no-nos that also include drugs, alcohol, spicy food, shellfish, and sushi. Notice I didn't mention chocolate.

Your husband will learn to be patient. This is good practice for any father-to-be. He will have to wait for you outside the restroom of every public and private establishment for the next nine months. He will also have to wait for you to go to the bathroom, not once, not twice, but three times before you leave the house, just to be sure you'll make it to the next stop. He will yell "fire," and you will still take ten minutes. Even so, he is likely to learn which gas stations have public bathrooms that you can access in a hurry, without the key attached to the metal plate marked with a skirt. And you will learn which ones are the most civilized.

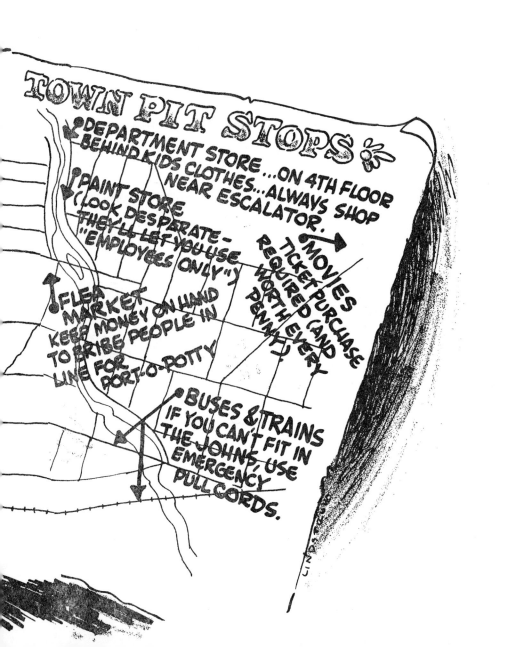

It gets worse. After about five months, you will need to carry an extra pair of panties with you. Any giggle and every sneeze will end with leakage. That's right—you who are awesomely creating an entire person within your frame can no longer control your own bladder. You can try kegeling, of course (those exercises to strengthen your muscles), but that's usually not the whole answer.

Never fear, there is a divine plan behind all this. Your body is teaching you not only how to survive on little or no sleep, but also how to nap and how to plan your day around something other than yourself. The good news is that your pit stops will end the instant that baby climbs off your bladder. The bad news is that then it will be the baby's turn. When you automatically wake up at 2:00 A.M. the first night of motherhood, you will contemplate the clock groggily, wondering why, after eighteen hours of exhausting labor, you are not sleeping. Seconds later, your baby will cry. Either she got used to your schedule, or it was really hers all along. Either way, every two hours for the next few months, when that glorious little bundle of joy cries, YOU WILL BE READY!

How to Break the News

Many women choose not to go public until they are past the first twelve weeks—the danger zone for early miscarriage. Yet often the first trimester is the roughest. Many of the early symptoms are good reasons for extra Tender Loving Care. When there's no bulging belly or other outward evidence of your raging hormones, no one is apt to give you a break. Don't run a full-page ad in the paper or mail announcements to everyone on your holiday card list, but do yourself a favor and tell those you spend the most time with. Here are a few suggestions:

To your husband: March into his office and interrupt an important business meeting, preferably in a glass-walled conference room. Be sure to stick around to watch him flounder. Then put on a sexy tube dress and take him to the most expensive restaurant in town for dinner. It may be the last time in years that you'll be able to do either.

To your mother: She already knows.

To your father: Your mother already told him.

To your sister: Give her your leftover tampons.

To your brother: Don't bother. He won't care until he sees the size of Junior's pitching arm.

To your friends: Go shopping and hint at the best shower presents.

To your boss: Wait until your insurance kicks in.

To neighbors: Ask them how their schedule looks next year for baby-sitting.

Scheduling Your Morning Sickness

I know a woman who woke up, showered, dressed, ate breakfast, threw up, and left for work every day for three months without being late once. Sound impossible? Here's how...

First of all, there is no guarantee when that nauseous feeling will reach the point of actually having to throw up. Nobody feels sorry for someone rolling down a waistband to air a queasy stomach, so don't think so negatively about morning sickness. Once you throw up, you feel MUCH better.

You are the only one who knows this, however, so feel free to mention humbly to your boss that you just heaved your cookies, and you will get special treatment. Enjoy it. In fact, I will go so far as to say that morning sickness is the perfect excuse for tardiness, as well as any social obligation you wish to avoid—much like the "no baby-sitter" excuse a year from now. Even your husband will catch on—I caught mine lying to an associate that he was taking care of poor sick me when he was really just catching an extra thirty winks. Believe me, I was happy to help. A rested husband is a scarce and valuable commodity.

However, don't overwork the morning sickness excuse, because there will be many occasions when you will have to use it in earnest. You see, morning sickness doesn't always happen in the morning. Not to fear. When you are going to vomit, like when you are going into labor, YOU WILL KNOW. As a general rule, be sure to avoid airplane and train travel and even unnecessary car rides. You never know how that speed bump will hit you. Always get a window. Beware of people who smoke and crowded places. Parties are particularly hazardous.

As soon as you learn you are pregnant, buy several cases of crackers. Stash crackers in your purse, your car, your desk, and, most importantly, on your nightstand. They really do absorb the acids and calm your stomach. Sometimes you will even get an extra ten minutes of peace before bolting to the toilet.

I found crackers a good way to build a rapport with a pet (who is likely to be at the end of the line for affection once the baby is born). After weeks of eating several crackers before getting out of bed, even gourmet water biscuits were incredibly unappetizing. I inhaled the first cracker. Then the second one would sit between my lips for a few moments as I summoned up the courage to take a bite. One day, my cat took this as an invitation to bite the other half—right out of my mouth. Since his mouth never touched mine, I was more impressed with his oral skill than annoyed. For the rest of my pregnancy, we broke our fast together in bed. Now that the baby's here, I rarely even pet him, and he is filled with arch resentment.

Down to business. Once morning sickness has firmly established itself, either in the first few months or the middle months of your pregnancy, you can try to control it. After the crackers allow you to get vertical, rush as fast as you can through your morning routine. Put on everything but lipstick. Since you probably don't have much of an appetite, but need that fuel to last until your first office snack, eat your peanut butter sandwich or granola bar very slowly. Then open the bathroom door, put a towel around your collar, and drink your juice. Now, count to ten. Voila! Automatic regurgitation. Cereal works the same way. Brush your teeth, apply lipstick, and you are on your way.

Note: In the interests of responsible reporting, I must say that there are some—in fact, many—lucky ones who sail through the entire nine months without a queasy moment, or whose queasiness lasts a very short time. You may be one of those. If so, congratulations—you lucked out!

Cosmetic Camouflage

By now, everyone you know has told you that you positively glow. Aside from the exciting prospects ahead, there is a biological reason to be "in the pink." Your heart is pumping a few extra pints of blood around that endless road map of tunnels inside you—and some get darn close to the surface. In fact, you may notice little red spots on your hands and your face. No, these are not spider or varicose veins (those you will find on your legs). These little beauty marks are from overactive blood vessels extremely close to the surface. Go ahead and press the spot with your thumb. Vanished for a moment, didn't it? It won't disappear for good until Junior relieves you of his vampire needs. Sometimes it will stay with you forever as a memento of this glorious experience. As soon as the baby was safely here, I had mine zapped by my dermatologist. Those forget-me-nots I can live without!

Some women have more than bulging veins during pregnancy. Many get blotchy and have skin ailments. Nearly everybody gets dark circles under the eyes. The key to a presentable self, of course, is make-up. Although your skin may require a little different chemistry in your base and your moisturizer, don't go crazy at the make-up counter. Concentrate on emphasizing your eyes and lips.

Even though magazines may suggest neutral shades of lipstick and eyeshadow to enhance that "earth mother" look, we know the truth: pregnancy requires a lot of make-up. It is much simpler and generally more flattering for those of us who are not models to simply brush on some powder and apply some dark mascara and a bright lipstick. With the limited options in maternity clothes, often your most exciting decision of the day will be between Red-Hot Rouge or Flower Power Pink.

Don't leave home without your lipstick. Many women recognize that they will never again be unburdened by a baby bag (not to mention a baby), so they refuse to carry even a purse during pregnancy. I was one of those women. Usually, I slipped the lipstick in my brassiere. Since few maternity bras are sexy, this little hidden treasure never failed to make me feel sexy—or at least sexier. When the weather was warm enough to melt a lipstick squeezed against my massive (for once) breasts, I found another solution. I made my husband carry it in his coat pocket. He didn't actually object, but he was concerned about what his buddies would think if he got hit by a car and they found lipstick in his pocket. So I wrote him an excuse note, just like in junior high. With my lipstick along, I looked great and he still felt macho. (Most men do feel pretty macho running around with a woman whom they impregnated!)

To whom it may concern:

Please note that the lipstick this man is carrying in his pocket is not his property, but his wife's. He has graciously volunteered to act as her purse so that she, now laden with the burden of pregnancy, need not be additionally burdened. Thank you for your understanding.

I Am Not YOUR Mother!

I don't care what Ronald Reagan called Nancy. Counselors say that one of the worst things for a marriage is for the wife to start acting like the husband's mother, SO DON'T TEMPT ME. It's bad enough that I'm the only one inclined to put his socks in the hamper.

As soon as your husband's partner knows that you are with child, he will start calling you "Mom"—or what is even worse, "Little Mother." If this happens first via the telephone, you will put down the phone and look around to see who he's talking to. AND THEN IT WILL HIT YOU. Since your husband is going to need all the cooperation—not to mention money— he can get over the next year, you will laugh charmingly and hang up as soon as possible. You have two options: either tell "Dad" to muster the diplomacy to nip this in the bud, or avoid talking to his partner for the next eight months.

There's not much else to say on this topic, except that all the changes in your life right now are overwhelming enough, so there's no need to rush into the "Mom" title. Or push it either. Okay, Buster?

When in Doubt: Accessorize

Maternity clothes are not known for being high fashion; they are known for being functional. Sometimes they are not even functional.

For warm weather, it would help if the clothing manufacturers would get in sync with the lingerie designers. "Maternity lingerie"—now THERE are two words that don't belong together. The only lacy maternity brassieres are those built for looks, not leverage. This, however irritating, is a minor point. Every pregnant woman knows that maternity bras are built bigger—all over. It's like strapping on a parachute harness (not that I ever will). The bras have half a dozen hooks in the back and the sides rise up to your armpits. Hence the problem: designers have never taken bras into account when creating armholes. This oversight can be expected for those cute little A-line numbers and baby-doll dresses, but when it comes to actual maternity styles, there is no excuse. I don't want my ugly bra to show, and I don't want to keep my arms pinned to my sides either. Natural stretch marks are bad enough—I am not about to aggravate the situation by allowing my unusually massive breasts to roam free. IS ANYBODY LISTENING OUT THERE? Not everybody likes wearing T-shirts under tank tops. And some of the cutest maternity clothes are summer rompers—sleeveless summer rompers. After weeks of deliberation, I solved this problem by cutting off the bottom of a LARGE stretch-lace teddy. Every outfit I wore had this adorable little lace "undershirt" showing. Tedious, but workable (until the size of my belly made the bottom of it roll up like a window shade).

Winter clothes are easier. Baggy sweaters can be found in your husband's closet, as well as in other, more expensive locations. The key is to get them so oversized that they hang down over your spreading hips. Later, when and if you get your waistline back, they'll hang long enough to belt.

Button-front nightshirts work great too, with the extra advantage of being useful for nursing. Either way, you can be incredibly fashionable with some trendy leggings. For a time you can even roll down the waistband of your old stretch pants and no one will know.

Face it, there comes a time in every woman's pregnancy when she must buy maternity pants. Try dark colors in soft, inexpensive, cotton knits. Forget those itchy sixty-dollar dungarees. You'll never wear them again—at least not until your next pregnancy.

Meanwhile, how do you keep the same six oversized tops from getting boring? Scarves. Big, colorful scarves. Here is your chance to be adventurous and learn how to tie the same scarf twenty-three different ways. Just make sure you leave some color hanging down to break up that enormous expanse of sweater. Long, clunky necklaces—the kind you usually avoid—can be plucked from your out-of-circulation-jewelry box and actually worn now, with good results. Another option is to string hard candies into chokers; you get fashion with a built-in snack.

Even if you have the budget and the need for expensive, pretty dresses, you'll still want something to flatter your face. Now is not the time to make an extreme change in hair style (unless your old one was a slicked-back duck tail). Which leads us to earrings. Take advantage of wild, crazy earrings now. Not long after Junior's arrival, you will have to give up all earrings except studs in order to keep your ears intact. For now, go to a flea market and pick up some big, junky ones. They don't have to last long; they just have to draw attention away from your bloated face.

Gloves can come in handy on formal occasions. With all the extra blood zooming around inside you, your hands and arms will look like road maps by the time you are in your third trimester. Many women have to remove their rings during pregnancy before losing their fingers—especially in the summertime. Wonder as much as you like about pregnant women without rings, but keep in mind that many of them ARE married.

Since EVERYTHING is growing during this time, some women swear by extravagant manicures. Then again, some don't want to attract any more undue attention to their limbs. Don't forget the hand model's trick of raising your fingertips heavenward. Your hands will look beautiful once again as the blood drains down. Unfortunately it is impractical to walk around with your arms up all the time—especially if you are like most pregnant women, whose regular deodorants are no longer working.

Remember, when you are pregnant, no one will notice or care that you wore the same thing last week. YOU will know, of course, but you know the answer:

Accessorize!

Battle of the Sexes

How do you feel when strangers place a hand on your bulging belly? Some pregnant women have a fit; others politely request its immediate removal. If the hand belonged to a woman, it didn't bother me so much. If it was a man's, the gesture was a little too intimate. This is pretty personal—after all, it's your belly. I do think, however, that for people to show interest is a good sign and represents hope for the future. We seem to feel a universal connection with the creation of a new life. Fortunately, most people only interfere in your personal space long enough to wager on your baby's sex.

I wish I had kept track of all the "tests" people used to determine the sex of my baby. There were action tests that involved which foot I stepped out with first or how I held my hands. There were observational tests too—some people swore they could tell just by looking at me.

My doctor, who has delivered 6,000 babies, felt that I did not need an amniocentesis, and he did not encourage unnecessary tests. These, he said, aside from high-risk pregnancies, were for young, nervous doctors who read the manual in one hand and deliver with the other. Since insurance companies are loath to cover unneeded expenses, I followed my doctor's advice. I could have had the test solely to determine my baby's sex, but I wanted the surprise. After all those months of pregnancy, there weren't many other secrets!

If your doctor suggests that you have the test and you discover the baby's sex, you'll have a lot more fun decorating the nursery. You won't be swimming in little yellow clothes after your baby shower. You can even call the baby by name in utero. But some doctors say you can't always be sure. EVERYTHING gets swollen with fluid—even the visual test can be misleading.

If you allow the sex of your baby to remain a mystery, you'll endure endless guessing games from people everywhere. Now I can't even remember who was right.

Decorating the nursery was a major challenge, since I happen to prefer pastels to primary colors. I figured I'd be sick of Mickey Mouse in a matter of weeks. We painted the room white and added a yellow-and-green border with sheep jumping over fences. Is that unisex enough for you? Then I held my breath and dressed the crib in a watercolor-flowered print. Jon reassured me that boys like flowers too.

Some people traditionally wait to have the furniture delivered until the baby is born, to be sure he or she is here and healthy, but I've never heard of this delayed method when it comes to gender-oriented sheets. Anyway, we had a girl's name, but we were still arguing over a boy's name during delivery. We had a little girl and the sheets are perfect. Does that mean I knew? Nope.

It's amazing how many choices you have. You can opt for drugs during childbirth or not, choose to nurse or not, work or not, find out the baby's sex or not. But the choice of whether to have a boy or a girl is not up to you. It's okay to have someone else make a decision for a change.

Things Your Doctor Never Told You

Your doctor has many patients, and he or she isn't necessarily aware of how much you know about the process of having a baby. The doctor's responsibility is to provide medical care and educate you about the important aspects of your particular pregnancy. It is your responsibility to ask as many questions as you think pertinent.

Although the wealth of informational books on how to have a healthy pregnancy and safe delivery can serve as a general background, it is still a good idea to learn your doctor's philosophies. Then you can explain your preferences. Aside from profound medical considerations, the doctor is bound to your wishes. You are, after all, the paying client. But don't be impatient if he or she has to cut short your visit or get back to you later on the phone because of an emergency—next time that emergency could be you.

Feel free to ask your doctor everything you want to know.

Remember:
The only stupid question is the one you don't ask.

Here are several not-so-pleasant details that you won't find in the manuals, your doctor won't think to tell you, your mother won't remember, and you may learn only by experience:

1. Even if you are blessed enough to avoid permanent stretch marks and get back to your pre-pregnancy weight, at least one part of your body will never be the same.

2. Your due date is at the END of the ninth month. Therefore the human gestation period is actually ten months. (My husband thought it seemed more like two years!)

3. They will force a catheter on you just prior to delivery. I swore to the nurse that I could manage by myself. She didn't believe me. She was right.

4. The second most painful experience related to childbirth is your first postpartem bowel movement.

5. Stopping your milk can be just as painful as starting it.

6. Even the extreme fatigue you feel during pregnancy is no preparation for the exhaustion a newborn brings.

Sex Appeal

The "bloom" of pregnancy has nothing to do with motherhood. It has everything to do with sex. Ever notice how it's always men who wax poetic about your sudden resemblance to a budding flower? Women say you look fine or you look great, but men say things like "radiant." Pregnant women are living proof of man's virility. Just the closeness of a pregnant woman can make a man blush. Men who don't like the full form of a pregnant woman are men who are uncomfortable with their own sexuality. After all, the sex inherent in the situation is unavoidable.

Women, on the other hand, have more difficulty feeling sexual during this time. Although it is fascinating watching your body take shape, the shape is radically different from the one you are familiar with. It is even more contrary to those found in the definitive physical dictionary of fashion magazines or *Playboy* (remember, those photos are airbrushed).

Take heart. If you are average, the first few months will see the emergence of a bombshell. It is not uncommon to lose ten pounds while your body starts sending all your food energy to that little blast furnace inside. Need I mention that morning sickness can greatly diminish your appetite? One area that will grow, no matter what, is your chest. My husband insists he saved four thousand dollars on a boob job while I reveled in my new cleavage. By the time my belly caught up, I could feel the baby moving. Those little butterflies give sex a new and wondrous meaning; you can feel the proof.

If you are already well endowed, or fall in a more zaftig range, pregnancy means nine months of freedom—freedom from worrying about your weight and freedom to eat whatever you want, within limits. You don't want to have to lose an extra thirty pounds on top of the first thirty pounds, right? Don't worry—when you are starving in your third trimester, heartburn will curb your appetite. It can be difficult, however, to eat as healthy as one would like with the tricky food aversions of pregnancy. The prenatal vitamin that your doctor will prescribe is the vital link between your mouth and a healthy baby. And there's always peanut butter.

Just remember, moderation in all things— even moderation.

Once you are overwhelmed with curves, enjoy every inch of it. It is all there for a purpose. Try to imagine what part of your baby is where. See that full thigh supporting the baby's tiny shoulder. Poke that puffy cheek and imagine the sustenance you are storing.

Have fun trying out different hugging positions with your husband. Hugs are very important these days. If you feel your belly is in the way, try a new approach. Consider that your baby is getting hugged, too. Hugging is now a warm, family event.

The same can be said for sex. You'll certainly need to experiment with positions. Don't forget that you are three making love now, and be gentle. Save the monkey sex for later—much later. Many women find that they are incredibly responsive during pregnancy. This is a definite bonus, so take advantage of it. Let your husband know what is going on with your body so that he doesn't get frightened or put off by anything unusual. You are pregnant because he wanted you. In all the fuss, don't forget that. He still wants you.

Erotic Massage

How does a pregnant woman spell heaven? M-A-S-S-A-G-E. All the pregnancy manuals agree that this is an ideal way to enlist your man's help. Not only will massage add a new dimension of intimacy, but also it will greatly alleviate any muscular aches and pains of pregnancy. It is delightful to have your belly and breasts massaged gently with oil. Since stretch marks are largely determined by your skin's natural elasticity, massage may not make a great deal of difference in the prevention department. It certainly helps to get your husband involved, however, and it does feel sexy and delicious.

Some people assume that massage is just another expensive way to be pampered. This is an extravagant falsehood. Soft tissue massage is a legitimate form of physical therapy for pregnant women. Massage helps to relax tight muscles and prevent undue strain and injury to your ligaments and joints. A pregnant woman carries an absurd amount of extra weight in one specific area. In order to balance this load, she leans back more, forcing her vertibrae to bunch together. Back strain is one of the most common complaints of pregnancy, and this discomfort in an area teaming with nerves seems to magnify every other ailment. Massage aids in circulation, and at the same time offers a relaxing antidote to the trials of a pregnant woman's day.

Many insurance policies include chiropractic care and cover massage therapy as a logical extension of that care. The policies that cover pregnancy as a "sickness" usually cover back problems as a result of that "sickness." For want of a better word, this term does allow pregnancy to be viewed as a state of health that is different from one's usual condition. This coverage generally lasts through a short postpartem period, until it is defined as "maintenance," which puts you back in your own pocketbook. Even if you are not covered, do yourself a favor and get an occasional massage. The physical and emotional rewards are far higher than the price.

The best way to find a licensed massage therapist, if not recommended by your doctor or chiropractor, is in any local baby newspaper. Some stores have their own newsletters, and some community newspapers have free parent news supplements. I was lucky enough to find a therapist who had a massage table with stretch material in the middle. Until then, pillows were the only answer to getting any applied pressure. This bed had adjustable collarbone and hip supports that enabled me to lie on my stomach for the first time in months. The only other way to lie this way is at the beach, with the sand carved out under you. Since we don't all have a beach, try to find someone with a table like this.

NOW FOR THE EROTIC PART. Every pregnant woman has a body part that cries out for stimulation. We're way past the G-spot here. It's more like an M-spot. "M" as in mmmmmmm. For me it was my feet. My major form of exercise during pregnancy was walking. Since the day the scale hit fifteen pounds above my norm (not quite the midpoint of my total gain), my feet were killing me. I'd go for a massage and my humor would improve, but not my feet. When I finally got my massage therapist to spend thirty minutes on my feet, I was in heaven. After the slightest bit of manipulation, I managed to get my husband into a nightly habit of rubbing my feet while watching television. I swear, it was the closest thing to the big O that I have ever felt. If anyone tries to tell you that foot massage isn't erotic, have her call me. Better yet, have her get pregnant and try it.

Baby Showers

Most people believe that a baby shower is an excuse to get presents. Practically speaking, it is. So make sure that your party isn't so elaborate that you would have saved money by just buying all the stuff yourself. Don't misunderstand me...parties are always fun, and it may be the last time you ever see your single friends. If, however, you've had a bridal shower and a wedding in the past few years, your friends may be fed up with all the fuss. So keep it simple.

I felt so bad about my friends having to spend money to fly to my wedding, that I didn't ask them to be in it, because then they'd have to buy the dresses (I regret this now). I bought my sister a nice simple dress with the theme of pink and pearls—something she could wear again. Out of related concerns, I had my own baby shower, so I wouldn't put anybody out. I spent a ton of money on food, favors, and trimmings. My mother did the cooking. Since it was the first baby shower I had ever been to, I have no complaints. It was great fun. We ate lunch and gossiped and guessed how big my waistline was and opened presents and party favors.

Several months later I went to a friend's baby shower at her neighbor's house. It was pot luck. We played a lot of silly games, and only the winners got party favors. (Those who were already mothers won the baby food guessing contest—you have to distinguish visually between different colors of mush—hands down.) This friend was a genius. She didn't have to spend money OR clean up.

All your friends want you to love their gifts. If your friends don't have children, help them out with suggestions. If you don't know what you need, ask another mother. When friends ask you directly, don't brush it off; be specific. If you know the baby's sex and tell your friends, you'll avoid getting whole wardrobes of little yellow or mint green neuter-suits. If the baby's a boy, it will save you from a dozen outfits with ruffles that have to be ironed and handmade designs with glitter that get all over the house (not to mention the baby).

Although people love to buy clothes, try to encourage group gifts, like a car seat or a stroller. You will need some clothes, of course, but people tend to buy cute-but-tiny clothes that modern, healthy babies grow out of in two weeks. Save some of the fun for yourself; buying clothes for your baby will be one of your first joyful postpartem activities when you finally get out of the house. This joy of shopping for your child will never end. The most bizarre part is that shopping for yourself won't be nearly as much fun as it used to be.

Other baby shower tips:

1. Have your shower early. It may not be as early as you think. It's nervewracking to be the focal point of a party with your suitcase packed and one eye on the door.

2. If possible, do something unusual—have a pool party, a barbecue, or a couples party.

3. If you've invited a struggling student or someone who can't spare the money for a gift, ask that person specifically for an afternoon or evening of baby-sitting. When the time comes, you'll appreciate this solution even more than your guest will now.

4. Beware of gift themes. I read about one Beverly Hills couple who learned that newborns are especially stimulated by the high contrast of black and white. Everything the baby received—at eight different showers— was black and white. Even the nursery motif was black-and-white cows. How does this baby get any rest?

5. Open the gifts as quickly as possible, so not to be blatant about the party's true purpose. Better yet, do it while your guests are eating, to avoid the long hushes likely to fall over circles of friends zeroed in on YOU opening.

6. Write thank-you notes immediately. You won't have time later, and besides, then there will be announcements to deal with. (Pick out your announcements and address the envelopes as soon as the gift thank-you's are out of the way.)

7. Relax and enjoy it. (Once the baby is here, relaxing will be harder and harder to do.)

Natural Childbirth Classes

Childbirth classes are wonderful. Although classes in the Bradley Method remain true to a policy of preparing you for natural childbirth, most LaMaze classes give you a good overview of all your options, including a variety of pain relievers. The abundance of biological information takes away a lot of your fears by explaining exactly what will happen in almost any case, including an emergency Caesarean section. I must admit that Jon and I opted to miss the demonstration films, so as not to undermine our new-found confidence.

The breathing techniques the classes teach are valuable, not only to help control pain, but also as a distraction.

Distractions are very important.

Birthing rooms are a great alternative to labor rooms, because you can listen to music or watch your favorite soap operas. Halfway through my labor period, my mother showed up and insisted on reading us short stories. At first I was annoyed, but gradually I became appreciative of anything that took my mind off the pain. It also distracted my husband from feeling so helpless—truth was, he was a big help with the breathing.

Do your homework for the classes, but don't panic about forgetting how to do the breathing exercises—most nurses are well schooled in LaMaze. If you are alert enough to recognize the start of a contraction, the breathing exercises truly help you maintain your equilibrium. If you don't feel the contraction until nearly its peak, do the breathing anyway and hang on for the ride.

The classes also tell you how great fetal monitors are. They are great, but don't rely on them. The external monitors loosen easily and are not always accurate. At one point during labor, my husband tried to reassure me by observing on the screen that this contraction was just a little one. It was the only time I swore during the whole process, and I vowed NEVER to trust him—or that machine—again.

Take the classes. Not only will you learn a lot from the instructor, but you'll also learn how other couples and mothers are handling this. You may even make some friends.

What? Me, Worry?

What's your biggest fear? I'll bet it has nothing to do with how big you may get, how good a mother you may be, or even how painful delivery might be. I'm sure the biggest fear for all mothers is that something may be wrong with the baby.

Many women don't make their pregnancy public until after the first three months, often because of the possibility of miscarriage, a quite common phenomenon. A good number of miscarriages take place before women are even aware that they are pregnant. Although a miscarriage understandably can be heartbreaking, try to take comfort in the knowledge that it is nature's way of saying there is something wrong. Try again.

With the extensive spate of tests available during prenatal care, usually you are able to know in advance if something is wrong. No doubt you've chosen your doctor carefully, or have known him or her for years, and you are learning everything you can about prenatal care. Now trust the doctor's judgment on what tests may be necessary for you.

The simple, routine tests that you are given during pregnancy can be a good indicator if anything is wrong.

That's why these visits to the doctor are so important. As long as you are taking care of yourself the best you can, there is nothing else you can do. So don't worry. After all, the odds are in your favor that the baby will be perfectly normal. And I mean PERFECTLY.

HOSPITAL HANDBOOK

Just Say Yes

According to my dictionary, a drug is "a substance used as a medicine." How a culture once so enamored of recreational drugs could have turned to natural childbirth as a righteous mandate, I'll never understand. There is a huge difference between "use" and the now common term "abuse." But abstinence from all painkillers may be overkill. I am not advocating that a woman be unconscious during delivery; I am simply suggesting that, with a little less pain, she may enjoy the miracle of birth a great deal more.

It is true that some women have incredible powers of concentration and can manage the pain of delivery drug-free. Others, especially after the first child, deliver easily with apparently little pain. If you are uncertain as to whether you will fit either description, don't let these women convince you that drugs are an evil tool for use only by weak-willed women.

When exploring alternative birthing methods, including water births and home delivery, I asked my obstetrician what he thought about birthing chairs. I had heard that by using these chairs (similar to the leg-lift stand at the gym), gravity could aid in the process. My doctor explained that it is muscle contraction, not gravity, that births the baby. Then he smiled and said that just because women had babies in the field a hundred years ago didn't mean I had to.

Fearing harm to the baby, many maternity ward staff members are loath to offer any kind of pharmaceutical relief until the last minute. Like most mothers I know, I was embarrassed to ask for painkillers until I was approaching the point of out-of-control behavior. I should have swallowed my pride and asked when the thought first hit me. In the meantime I swore off having additional children unless by adoption or simple fission. Even after fifteen hours of intense back labor, I had to beg my nurse to call my doctor to prescribe a shot. Believe me, I have NEVER begged for a shot before. And that measly little thing didn't result in anything other than a little red dot on my rump.

After months of research, I had decided that if I needed it, I would opt for an epidural (a regional nerve block). This was the advice Christina Ferrare offered after the Los Angeles television audience watched her entire pregnancy, day by day. And after all those babies, she ought to know.

The only bad part about an epidural is that they won't even order it until you are halfway dilated. Those first few centimeters can take an excruciating amount of time. After twenty hours, I reached the breaking point and they called the anesthesiologist. I watched the clock for another hour until he showed up. The fact that they had to stick a needle in my back— and leave it there—didn't diminish my enthusiasm for the shot in the least. The pain lessened—some. I whined and cajoled the doctor into another dose. Once the drug took effect, I promised to name my baby after him if it was a boy. The epidural numbed the pain, yet I still felt every contraction and remained in control of the pushing. I will never forget that saintly man. Fortunately, I had a girl.

Finally, a more general word about pain...There is great controversy over whether women experience more pain and endure it better than men. Kidney stones are rumored to be men's greatest pain, but never has history reported a man to have passed an eight-pound kidney stone. My husband argues that it is all relative to the size of the porthole. We will never know.

Our saving grace is that pain has no memory. Even between contractions, I couldn't really remember HOW it felt, except by recalling the metaphor that occurred to me in the throes of labor—of sitting on a gas burner while someone kept adjusting the flames higher. Even after the delivery, I couldn't remember the actual sensation of the most intense pain. Indeed, less than a week later, I retracted my pain-induced prophesy of no more babies and admitted that I'd do it again.

My doctor sides with women in the pain endurance contest. He believes that if men had children, not only would pregnancy and childbirth be the most exalted activity on earth, but also that the human race would die out in two generations.

Queen for a Day

The day you have a baby, you are the Queen. The day you leave the hospital, you are History.

Fifty years ago, childbirth rated a good ten days in the hospital. By then the mother would be recuperated enough to take on the heavy demands of a newborn, and any health problems of mother or baby would be taken care of early. Nowadays, generous insurance companies typically cover three days in the hospital—including labor and delivery. Caesarean patients usually get an extra forty-eight hours. An alarming number of companies not only require extensive waiting periods to qualify for pregnancy coverage, but also charge an additional premium. So many people are not covered by insurance that most hospitals offer a popular bargain rate for twenty-four-hour maternity patients. Not surprisingly, reports show that the number of postpartum infections and lingering infant ailments has skyrocketed.

This current state of affairs would be more acceptable if every new mother had a bountiful support system to help her out at home. As it is, the extended family is no longer commonplace in our society. Relatives who might lend a hand or two often live clear across the country. Paid help is difficult to find and often unaffordable. Even if the new father can stay home to help, circumstances are sometimes desperate. HAVING A BABY IS A MAJOR ORDEAL. The fact that so many people do it doesn't make it any easier. The mother will be exhausted and generally still in a great deal of discomfort. With the onset of breast milk—sometimes painful—and the depletion of whatever physical resources remain by nursing every two hours, a new mother discovers that the lack of sleep caused by a crying baby is overwhelming. Add hormonal changes and the realization of parental responsibility to the emotional landscape, and post-partem depression is not a surprising phenomenon.

At the hospital, the nurses volunteer to do the diaper changing—let them. Although it is currently in vogue to keep the baby in your room at all times, ask them to keep the baby at night so you can get some precious rest. Remember, in all cases, YOU ARE THE BOSS. If you are nursing, they will wake you every few hours whether you like it or not. Feel free to instruct them to skip a nursing session. They have plenty of glucose water to sustain the baby. Be sure to take advantage of the last time you will eat regular meals for months. You need the fuel. It is also the last time you will eat anything hot for a long time.

In addition, being in the hospital keeps you from energy-intensive work, like laundry, cleaning, birth announcements, and thank-you notes. Nurses or aides are there whenever you need help breast-feeding, walking, and going to the bathroom. If you ask them, they can save your husband from making ten trips a day to the pharmacy for pain relievers, sanitary napkins, and stool softeners. If this extra service costs you a bit more, it will usually be worth every penny. The same financial philosophy holds true for getting private rooms... maybe even more so. If at all possible, do it. Your own nursing and guest schedule, not to mention your personal hygiene practices, are hard enough to cope with. Add a roommate's, and the situation will be more than twice as hectic.

After all the months of build-up, a lot of new mothers are in a rush to get home and really start being a mom. If you remember anything in this book, let it be this: even if your Prince Charming is a devoted father and you will return to work in six weeks with a live-in nanny...

...motherhood is like an endless game of tag and you are IT!

Visitors

The first thing you will want to do after the baby is born is shout from tall buildings that a miracle has happened. Or, you might just want to phone everyone you know in the world. If you've made up a list of people to call, this will be easy. The gist of your announcement over the phone is remarkably similar to the "name, rank, and serial number" used to identify military personnel. Those you call will want to know the baby's sex, name, and weight.

If they remember to ask how you are feeling, DON'T tell them the truth. Just say, "Thrilled." This way, they'll share your happiness by sending you lots of flowers and you can get all your calls out of the way in time to receive guests in person.

Most hospitals discourage visitors other than close family, especially if the baby is in your room. Ostensibly, this is to avoid unnecessary germs from the outside. It is also to give you a chance to rest. Take advantage of the rest part.

When you get home, the fun begins. You invite everybody, and they all come. After watching you go through that interminably long pregnancy, who can resist viewing a miracle? They will be proper guests and will try not to stay too long. You will hush them when they try to get you some water and you will make them ice tea. You will all be amazed at how well you are doing. You will try to avoid straightening up the place and laundering your nightgowns, but you will do it anyway. Your body will remember to take a nap, but you will be having too much fun. You will go on for days and days like this until everyone has seen the baby. Then they will be gone. Your husband will go back to work. You will have to resume grocery shopping, cooking, and cleaning. YOU WILL COLLAPSE.

Essentially, there are only two things to remember about having guests: 1) avoid having too many too soon, and 2) accept every bit of help that is offered.

Spitting Image

Who does the baby look like? I'll never forget an interview I saw on television recently. A new father, Mr. Smith, was explaining how his parents couldn't get over how much the baby looked like them.

Everything—the eyes, the mouth, the forehead—it was all Smith. In fact, they were so impressed by the family resemblance that they were embarrassed for the mother's family, the Joneses.

When the two families met in the hospital they exchanged only cursory compliments. When the Smiths left, the Joneses pulled the father aside and apologized profusely for sounding rude. They were so sure the baby looked exactly like a Jones that they didn't know what to say to the Smiths.

Newborns are a lot like modeling clay. Even the coloring can change. Also, descriptions change to match the convictions of the beholder—not unlike someone pointing at your belly, bulging with life, and claiming that it is a boy, FOR SURE. As in the fable of the emperor and his invisible clothes, most people will agree with the initial "looks like" proclamation.

A month after my baby was born, I was very upset that she seemed to look so much like her father. She already had his last name. Her middle name was my mother's, and her first name was her own. After all the time and effort I put into having her, I felt cheated. I wanted her to look like me. After growling for a few weeks, I looked again. She DID look like me—for a few days, anyway. I recently took her back to see my old high school friends. They were pretty divided on which parent she looked like.

It takes a few years to sort things out, looks-wise. So enjoy every stage, take lots of pictures, and don't worry who the baby looks like (unless it's the milkman).

Not Just Another
Pretty Chest

Breast-feeding isn't for everyone. If you're not comfortable with it, how do you think your baby will feel? So, if YOU're really not up for this messy ordeal, don't be guilt ridden. Be relieved. You don't have to! After all, our mothers' generation was taught that nursing was déclassé, and we all turned out all right, didn't we? Well, didn't we?

If you do want to nurse, that's great. Breast-fed babies are reported to have fewer incidences of colds and infections when they are living directly off of your antibodies. But some experts say that most of the nutritional benefits are depleted after the first month of nursing. And after three months, 97 percent of what you have to offer, besides food, has been utilized. The longer you go on with breast-feeding, the more food they get, but the antibodies decrease with time. Then, of course, the babies have to catch up and build their own antibodies. Some women nurse for the pleasure. Some nurse to save money on formula. Formula is expensive, but it's also very good nourishment for babies who don't nurse full-time or who stop before they are old enough for cow's milk.

As for when to start baby on solid food...my doctor told me about a study done somewhere with one hundred babies who nursed exclusively for one year, and another hundred babies who drank formula exclusively for one year. They were all just as healthy as those babies who started on food at eight months. I tried to explain that to my mother, who, like many grandmas, was shoving real food—including ice cream—down my baby's throat before she could crawl. My baby was strictly on formula at that point. Why hassle with food before I had to, I figured? I told my mother that, if she didn't stop, she couldn't see the baby next week. True power comes with motherhood.

Every mom's experience is different: different from what you expect, and different from other moms' experience. I had originally planned to nurse for six months, until my baby got teeth. Due to an illness that refused to quit without both medication and energy conservation (mine), I quit after three months. I'm sure that I missed it more than my baby. She'd drink anything if she was hungry enough. I admit, however, that it was nice to let my husband feed her for a change. And she got her first two teeth at four months, so it was just as well.

Nursing, like childbirth, is a universal act with a lot of variables. If you are totally psyched about it, take a class. If you are the least bit nervous about it, read a book. The La Leche League has plenty of publications about this wondrous exchange between you and your baby. Remember, the

League elevates this basic ritual to the level of a holy and complicated art. Get the facts, but don't be too concerned about following this doctrine past the point of comfort. You do not have to nurse until your child is eighteen—or even eighteen months.

The bottom line is that babies suck instinctively. Nurses can show you how to accommodate them easily. Don't expect the nurse to be sympathetic when your milk is slow coming in—or drying up. For that, you'll be better off just applying hot towels. A nurse's job is to provide care that promotes health. His or her motive for helping you nurse is to make sure that your little baby gets enough to eat. Take advantage of this professional knowledge. Remember to use this professional experience as a guideline—not a rule—for your particular situation. YOU are in control.

Here are some things the nurse probably won't tell you:

1. Breast-feeding is messy. You will have more wet spots on your bed than you did when you tried to get pregnant.

2. You should always wear a bra for support.

3. Get used to eating your dinner cold. No matter when your dinner is ready, Junior will be hungry. We implemented the "baby food chain" at our dinner table: I fed the baby while my husband fed me. We still use this method. Only now my husband feeds the baby while I feed him.

4. You can nurse in public just as easily as in private, if you are comfortable and dressed appropriately. Generally your family and friends—even your husband's friends—will take their behavioral cues from you. You may experience more direct eye contact than usual. Or, you may have truly interested observers. After all, it's not every day that people get to see beautiful breasts doing what they're made for.

5. Whatever you decide to do, enjoy it. It's your body and your baby. Pretty thrilling, isn't it?

Sleep

Remember how you used to fall deep asleep, slumbering through the late show, the alarm, and minor earthquakes? By the time you are reading this, you have said good-bye forever to sleep as you know it. This is not to say that you will never sleep again: you will. Not for many months, of course, but you will.

People often ask if I use a baby monitor at night. No need, I tell them, my personal monitor is always on. My husband and I wake up at her every sniffle, burp, and sigh. We wait nervously to see if it will grow into something that merits our attention, and, if it doesn't, we gratefully fall back into our REMs. Until the next noise.

We like to have her in bed with us in the morning to play. Sometimes, on a bad night when she won't be comforted, we move her to our bed. But I can't sleep with her there. Every breath reminds me that she is next to me and I must watch out for her. Finally, when I'm so overwhelmed by exhaustion that I'm ready to doze off, it's dawn and she is up for the day. How can I be mad at that chirpy little beauty. She's happy—it's time to play, time for Ma-ma.

Being a mom is definitely a drag when it comes to sleep. But, then again, when else do you get to be a guardian angel?

Bonding

Are you sick of this word yet? Whether we're talking about parenting or any other kind of interpersonal relationship, *bonding* is the buzz word of our times. There is little debate over the importance of bonding, yet the application varies with experts from Brazelton to White. My husband insists that the term comes from the root word of Bondo, as in glue. If only it were that easy.

Once the umbilical cord is cut, an intimate parent-child relationship is vital to a child's well-being. We can follow this reasoning, along with the child, into adulthood. As an avid career woman, I used to pride myself on never having changed a diaper and having successfully avoided small children. When I was finally ready to join Club Mom, my husband was understandably concerned. Not to worry. If you are happy about the prospect of motherhood, maternal instincts will make you comfortable with your baby, no matter how her head is shaped when she enters the world.

If you cannot help being unhappy about your pregnancy, please seek family counseling. Don't be afraid; be proud that you have recognized a potential problem and are dealing with it in a positive way. Bonding is all about love and security. It is about an emotional connection that is so strong it ultimately results in a child's confident independence and adulthood. Healthy attachment leads to healthy separation.

According to my mother (who is a therapist with a Ph.D. in child development), the latest rage in "pop" therapy is testing and treatment for an old problem with a catchy new name: Attention Deficit Disorder—ADD, for short. A parent can pay a lot of money to find out that the reason a child has a short attention span, learning disabilities, or general unease, is that she never properly bonded with her parent(s). Many adults learn this about themselves while in therapy for a more tangible problem. The no-bonding problem may only be a symptom. Perhaps the baby was unwanted, or perhaps she was supposed to be a boy. Perhaps she simply lived at a different pace from her mother's. Parental apathy can be unconsciously communicated through a lack of true intimacy as simple as a mother not wanting to hold the baby. Babies are smart. They, like you, can tell if you love them or not. And if they can't trust your love, how can they love themselves? How can they love someone else?

Early bonding is the goal of those who encourage pregnant women to talk to their animated bellies. Flashcards and symphonies have nothing to do with this. Many believe that all your warm, positive thoughts are carried from your brain through the umbilical cord to the baby. There have been studies that show how unhappy pregnant mothers, those who feel apathetic, and especially those undergoing stress or emotional trauma, are more likely to have colicky babies. So, TRY TO BE HAPPY. It can't hurt.

Many hospitals now encourage early bonding by giving the baby to the mother immediately upon delivery. What mother can resist loving a miracle in her arms? My nurse encouraged me to breast-feed at that moment as well. Although it is not necessary to have the baby with you every second of every day from there on out, MORE IS DEFINITELY BETTER. The same goes for the father. Simply because his body hasn't been very involved in the process doesn't mean the baby can't become just as attached to him.

Babies are utterly dependent. They learn quickly to depend on you—if you let them. They love you unequivocally. Love them back, and you'll keep their love. It's as simple as that.

Experts tell us that the FIRST THREE YEARS of life are the most developmentally important years. These are the years in which we learn all the major motor activities. These years provide the basis for our intellectual growth. We learn how to deal with our emotions, other people, and the world around us. Therefore, a human's personality is pretty complete by age three. Will she be a leader or a follower? Aggressive or shy? Will she be able to reason ethically? Will she have the capacity to trust—and to love? A baby learns all these things primarily from those who take care of her from that very first day of life. In terms of actual development, a tiny baby overcomes the greatest obstacles right at the start, then expands her knowledge as her mind and body become fine-tuned.

For this reason, many child development specialists believe that the period of the first few months is the most important time for bonding. Some extend that period to one year. Others insist that the first three years are equally important. Illogically, I happen to agree with all these experts. Bonding is so important that I would not set an endpoint, lest people assume that after that point it's okay to stop. It definitely gets harder to stay with the program, especially for working or otherwise busy parents, as a child gets older. But a family that starts out strong has a better chance of holding up under outside influences.

After all, it's a cold, cruel world out there. Don't we want our children dressed in the warmest coats possible?

Going Solo

Are you a single mother? If so, be patient with the nurse's prying questions, as well as everyone else's. When people assume that there is a "mister" waiting to take you home from the hospital, try to understand that they want the best for you. The ideal family does include two parents. That is undoubtedly one reason why it takes two to make a baby. And making the baby is the easy part.

Perhaps you realized that the natural father wasn't right for you—or for fatherhood. Perhaps, like most of us, you grew up considering motherhood as something to do LATER—and now is as late as it gets. The big plus about having a baby without a mate is that this often is a baby of CHOICE. You have CHOSEN to have and keep this baby. He or she will enter the world loved—and that is at least half the reason for a happy childhood.

Club Mom is the largest club in the universe—and you, single or married, are a welcome member. Call your neighbors with the news BEFORE you leave the hospital. Invite them to see the baby when you get home. Married moms will be happy to help you if you let them know what you need—from tips on buying baby clothes to an hour or two of companionship. When they ask if there's anything they can do for you now, tell them a tuna casserole would be heavenly. Don't cringe—it will be. If you just left an all-consuming job, a neighbor can introduce you to other mothers in the area. You'll be surprised at how many there are. They are sure to know other single moms.

If you're interested, maybe your neighbor even has an eligible cousin. (Don't worry, your being a mother will not put off Mr. Right. Instead, it may bring out a warm, nurturing side of you that might have been hidden at the office.) You know how babies are scene-stealers in the movies? It's also a fact of everyday life. EVERYONE LOVES BABIES. Your baby will be your entree into the largest society there is. Take advantage of this. It's a lot of fun.

There are thousands of moms who either start out single or become single by one means or another. This is a vast support system that will be vital, not only to your survival, but to your happiness. Take your beautiful baby for a stroll as soon as you are both up to it. Just by walking around your neighborhood or shopping with the baby, you will meet many women. Start by inviting another mom to walk with you. Invite a mom at the park for tea. Invite several moms and babies over to watch a funny video. It won't matter if you miss most of the movie. Many of the despondent single moms my mother counsels in therapy are revitalized by this nurturing contact.

One of the best things that you can do for your baby is to be happy—often the hardest thing of all to do. So, do something for yourself this week; get a sitter and have your hair cut or go out to lunch. Most of all, be proud of yourself and your baby. You are doing great! Despite the increased responsibility and hardship...

...you will never regret your decision to have a baby.

Your former family of pets may regret this decision, but you won't. Being single is no reason to miss the goosepimply joy of having your baby hug you and say "Ma-ma" for the first time.

YOU KNOW YOU'RE A MEMBER OF CLUB MOM WHEN...

- you automatically like anyone who's nice to your baby
- you actually ask your mother for advice
- strange women tell you their life stories
- you avoid looking in mirrors
- "getting out" means into the back yard
- your biggest file is "restaurants that deliver"
- intimacy means three in a bed
- all you want for your birthday is sleep
- headphones are a thing of the past

LIFETIME
MEMBERSHIP
GUARANTEED

Now What?

Can you believe they let you take your baby home without some kind of license? They hand you this tiny morsel of life in its most critical stage, and trust that you can nurture it. Lack of a strong, geographically convenient family unit has made the vocabulary of infant care as alien a language as Ancient Celtic. And our educational system has not yet met this need for family education. Even if you read every book, watch every videotape, and spy on every mother you know, taking care of the baby will still be a huge and mysterious adjustment.

Don't despair. Trust your instincts. All the baby wants now is to get back inside you. All you can do to help is hold the baby as much as possible, feed her whenever she's hungry (or on a schedule, as you like), and keep her warm and dry.

You will see the pediatrician every few days at first, so keep a list of questions to ask at your next visit. Call your pediatrician's office at the slightest concern. The nurse is your lifeline. Usually, she can take care of any worries you may have; if she doesn't know the answer she can get one from the doctor faster than you can if you wait for the doctor to call you back between appointments. If you haven't already, meet all the other doctors in the office so that you will feel comfortable speaking with whoever is on call at 3:00 A.M.

Your mother will be helpful, but not as helpful as a friend or neighbor who has toddlers. Mothers love to share advice, so don't worry for a moment that you are being a pest by asking for it. Mothers no longer merit the respect in this society that they deserve, so they love to share the joys and miseries with others who can relate—really. Just keep in mind that every mother has her own way of handling her children. As you listen to all this maternal counsel, you'll find it easy to separate style from substance—and come to your own conclusions.

It is normal to be exhausted. Don't be angry at your newborn for crying so much. The baby is exhausted, too. If this is all new and strange for you, imagine what it must be like for that tiny, helpless little creature. Many times, you'll check to see that the baby is fed, dry, warm—and still she will cry. It could be from colic or from too-tight pajamas or maybe from nothing at all. All you can do is comfort the baby and wait it out. Get as much rest as possible, so your patience doesn't wear thin.

A baby cannot get too much loving. Neither can a mother. It's the start of a wonderful mutual admiration society.

Nature vs. Nurture
Nature is beyond your control.
Concentrate on nurture.

Best Bets for Bed

You already know how to arrange six pillows so that you can sleep comfortably in your ninth month. (Of course, you really didn't sleep at all during your ninth month, but at least you knew how to do it comfortably.)

Now that you are one again, bedtime can be just as tricky. If you are nursing, you still can't sleep on your belly; it's not only painful, but very messy. You can try to sleep on your side, but you're still mashing one boob. (At least your sinuses are unblocked and you can breathe again.) The best way to sleep is on your back—with one of those infamous pillows under your knees for back support. Remember the waterproof liner you put under your sheets in case your water broke in the middle of the night? Put it back—you may roll over, press a bosom, and flood the bed with nature's finest.

While the baby is in your room, sleep on the side of the bed closest to the crib. Eventually, you'll learn to nurse lying down, and you can doze off at the same time. Just don't get too comfortable and smoosh her. When the baby is moved into another room, CHANGE SIDES! Make sure you sleep on the side of the bed that is farthest from the nursery. Let your husband get up for a change. This is especially important when the baby is on the bottle. This maxim may sound too simple to be true, but I guarantee it will save you from plenty of moonlight excursions. All you have to say is, "Honey, you go, please? You're closer." If he pretends to snore, you snore louder. He can't stand the crying any more than you can.

One last thing. Most babies' first sound is "da-da." Your husband will certainly interpret this as a word. Not just any word, but his name. Let him believe this. Encourage the fantasy. Then, when your baby wakes up at night and makes those sounds, your husband will think the baby is calling him. He'll be only too thrilled to answer in person. You may never have to get up again.

Infancy conforms to nobody;
all conform to it.

—Ralph Waldo Emerson

Whose Body Is It, Anyway?

Repeat after me, "My body is an alien. My body is an alien. My body is an alien." Okay, now you can look in the mirror. Eeeeaaaarrrgggh!

If you looked in the mirror before preparing yourself for the fact that your body is beyond your control, then heaven help you. The long months of pregnancy are difficult enough, but at least then there is a goal in sight and lots of books to help you along the path to hugeness. There are fitness videos to get you back in shape. There are even audio cassettes on avoiding postpartum depression as it relates to unmet expectations and raging hormones. But there is not a clue as to what your body might look like once it is all you again.

View your body as an experiment in biology. If you were in good shape before your pregnancy, and it was your first, you will probably bounce right back. We are talking about weight, not muscle tone. You will still be soft. Even if you can see the vertical ridges around where your stomach muscles used to be, when you crawl on all fours to retrieve that silver rattle, your belly may find it before you do.

Think of it this way— you can see your toes again. And your maternity clothes never looked better. Don't they look great? Keep those jeans in the drawer for a while. By the way, did you see that woman leave the hospital in pants? Was she crazy, or what?

If you are nursing, you are doubly blessed. Not only can you hold up that sexy bustier without cotton padding, but the sheer bulk of your chest makes your shrinking waistline look tiny by comparison. This is especially helpful since your waistline may stop shrinking a few inches short of your old juniors pant size. Face it, with motherhood come misses-sized pants. (You like those even numbers better anyway, right?) If you are already overly endowed in the chest department, you will feel positively petite in the future. It's really a can't-lose situation.

As for that extra roundness, my husband likes to tell me how feminine it is. HIS extra roundness, of course, is a sign of contentment. Mine, to be honest, is more an indication of a change in priorities. Once you are a mom, going to the gym drops about fifteen notches on your list. Besides, you walk a lot behind the baby stroller. You don't have to compete anymore. Everyone's going to be looking at the baby, anyway. That's no excuse for eating hot fudge sundaes every day, but what's the harm in once or twice a week?

So, give yourself a few months and appreciate the ordeal your body has been through before you try to whip it back into shape. Consider it a shrine, a temple of creation. Whose body is it, anyway?

Simplifying Your Beauty Routine

The best way to simplify your beauty routine is to throw out all your make-up. If you must, save some base coat and rouge for special occasions.

On a day-to-day basis, you'll find that if you get the chance to wash your face at all, slapping on some moisturizer will be an extravagance. Once you get in the swing of things and venture out in public, go easy on yourself. Just brush on some powder. Your baby doesn't care if you are wearing mascara. Neither does the lady at the grocery check-out. Put it on for your husband if you want, but remember that he's now seen you under much worse conditions, so it really doesn't matter.

Put make-up on if it makes you feel good; that's the ONLY reason worth your time.

Don't Leave Home Without It

Babies are very portable. You need to get out of the house, and they love new stimulation. Whether you are visiting friends or shopping, there are certain things you should always bring with you.

First six months (in order of importance):

1. Patience
2. Sense of humor
3. Diapers and changing accessories
4. Pacifier, preferably with leash attached to baby's shirt
5. Full bottle or cover-up for nursing, plus nursing pads and burp cloth
6. Toys—car keys and unbreakable bracelets are suitable substitutes
7. Kleenex
8. Baby blanket
9. Additional outfit for baby—handy after a major spit-up
10. Spare top for you—same reason as above

11. Doctor's phone number, teething ointment, baby Tylenol
12. Wallet—just driver's license and credit card would be easier still
13. Dark sunglasses (to cover red, tired eyes)
14. Lipstick—it might not help the way you look, but it will make you feel better

Over six months:
1. Everything listed above, plus Cheerios

You Are Not Alone

You are sitting on your couch feeding your five-week-old baby, numbly clicking through the TV soaps. Yesterday your baby smiled at you for the first time. You were so thrilled, you finally made that tough decision to stay home and infuriate your boss for life. Your friends are all still at work, and though you are happy, you are lonely.

You are not alone. Once you leave the working world, you will find that the rest of the universe is geared toward children. Other new moms will love your company. Even moms of toddlers will love your company; they already miss holding a baby.

An informal way to meet other moms during the difficult first few months is to take long walks with your baby. (If your child's infancy coincides with below-zero winter months, push her around a shopping mall.) Other moms do the same thing. It's definitely THE most popular form of exercise. When you come across another mom-and-stroller, don't be shy. You can always ask what time it is.

Another great way to meet moms is at the park. Even though your baby can't crawl yet, she will love to watch the other humans close to her own size, and it will be relaxing for you. At least three moms will ask you how old your baby is. If they don't, feel free to ask about their kids, in the guise of seeking developmental information. It is a sure ice-breaker.

Or, if you see other mothers with babies at the pediatrician's office, ask the nurse for their names and numbers. She'll probably check with them first, but she'll be happy to matchmake. Even if you don't see other moms while you are there, the nurse can probably refer you to a few. I invited a few such acquaintances over with their babies one morning, and we had a great time comparing notes. For those first few months, we rotated houses and met when it was convenient. Now that my daughter is mobile and can play more around older neighborhood children, we don't see each other as often. But it was fun while we needed it.

Once you and the baby are out of the woods, you'll be surprised at the number of children's activities in your area. Many malls have children's entertainment once a week in the form of a clown, a magician, or a storyteller. Mall stores may give out balloons and door prizes. Libraries have reading hours for children. Your baby probably is too young to enjoy these things, but, again, she will definitely love to watch the other children. Babies love babies. And you'll meet other moms (sometimes even dads).

There are more formal mother-and-child groups, such as "Mommy and Me" classes, offered at local recreation centers, colleges, churches, and through other organizations. These all vary in price and quality, so sit in on a class before signing up. Some are for you and your baby at three months, some at six months, some at a year or older. So no matter where you live, you are not alone. In fact:

You will never be alone again.

Pacifiers Are for Pacifying

There is a great brouhaha over the use of pacifiers. Some people think babies get too dependent on them. Some think that it is a good way to avoid thumb-sucking.

Face it, babies need to suck. They don't need to suck on you or on a bottle all the time. Many babies become adept at sucking in their sleep, without a pacifier...a sweet sight. Some babies won't even take a pacifier.

My hospital gave my baby an orthodontically correct pacifier right from the start. Not to trick her out of dinner and not to shut her up, but to do what it's intended for: pacify her. After all, babies go through an ordeal just being born. When they are a little older, a pacifier gives them something to play with. If you are away from home and the baby is at the stage where everything goes in her mouth for exploration, a pacifier can be the safest choice. As babies begin to make sounds and words, they will generally wean themselves naturally from a pacifier. It's hard to talk with something in your mouth! A pacifier is the perfect thing to give a fussy baby at night when you need some sleep . Many babies go to sleep with a bottle. This should be discouraged to prevent tooth decay.

We must have bought fifty pacifiers in the past year, and I can find only two of them now. Wait...there's one under the couch! Make that three. Pacifier clips are enormously handy. Not only do they prevent dropping and losing pacifiers in the grocery store, but also they provide the baby with instant access when you are busy comparing oatmeal prices.

Doctors agree that if a pacifier falls on the ground, DO NOT PUT IT IN YOUR MOUTH to clean it. Your mouth is a minefield of germs that your baby may not be immune to. If you can't handily rinse off the pacifier under a faucet, give it back to the baby anyway. Don't be paranoid—regular dirt probably won't hurt them. My husband's late Scottish grandmother used to say that you have to eat a pound of dirt before you die. Most healthy babies have a good start at this.

I have heard of two effective ways to break an older child of the pacifier habit. The first is to hold a ceremony—the child throws it in the trash. When she asks for it later, she can be reminded that SHE threw it away. She will remember this rite of passage, and accept the loss as a big girl. Another approach is to wait until your child happens to lose her pacifier—perhaps at the park, the pool, or a friend's house. Throw away the rest of the pacifiers and remind her that she lost it. She will remember and eventually accept it.

People who hate pacifiers often think of them as devices for frustrated mothers to shove into their screaming children's mouths. Remember, one dictionary definition of "pacify" is "to calm; to bring or restore to peace; to soothe." We can all use a little soothing from time to time, don't you agree?

Adam and Eve had many
advantages,
but the principal one was that
they escaped teething.

—*Mark Twain*

Is There Sex After Childbirth?

It's not like riding a bicycle. You remember how, but you can't just hop on and pedal. After all the months of mystery, this is one area in which most doctors do have all the answers. To avoid infection, wait until six weeks after the birth of your baby. To make up for the absence of certain hormones while nursing, use lubricant. Listen to your doctor.

A typical scenario:

NEW MOM and NEW DAD are on the couch reading. NEW DAD puts down his newspaper and stretches back luxuriantly, resting his eyes. NEW MOM flips restlessly through her magazine.

NEW MOM: (fishing) Guess what day it is?

NEW DAD: Tuesday.

NEW MOM: No, that's not what I mean.

NEW DAD: It's not our anniversary, is it?

NEW MOM: No...

NEW DAD: Not your birthday—not your mother's birthday—not my mother's birthday—not Mother's Day…

NEW MOM: That's always on a Sunday.

NEW DAD: Right. Well, let's see…our taxes are paid, it's not Christmas Eve. I give up.

NEW MOM: It's the baby's birthday!

NEW DAD: That was a quick year! I could swear he was just born about—oh, say—six weeks ago.

NEW MOM: (turns over, sits up) That's right, six weeks.

NEW DAD: (light bulb goes on) Aha! Six weeks as in…

NEW MOM: As in we're legal. I can't believe it's been sixteen weeks since we…

NEW DAD: (interrupting—groans) I can. I was amazed we made it through the last ten weeks before your due date!

NEW MOM: We didn't, remember?

NEW DAD: Oh, right. (smiling) How can I forget? Except that it seems like so long ago. Thank goodness the baby was early.

NEW MOM: Okay, so it's been thirteen weeks.

NEW DAD: Ninety-one days.

NEW MOM: (suggestively) Shall I get comfortable?

NEW DAD: Uh, darling, why don't we make this an occasion? I could get some thick steaks and Rigaud candles and red roses and a little Ravel's "Bolero."

NEW MOM: What do we need all that for?! (crushed) You just don't want to.

NEW DAD: No, sweetheart, that's not it. What's another day? (beat) All right, I admit it—I'm really tired. He was up four times last night.

NEW MOM: I remember. You don't think I'm tired? You just pushed paper all week. I got drooled on, puked on, pooped on…This is the first time today he's been down for more than twenty minutes.

NEW DAD: I know it's a lot of work. If I had breasts I'd stay home for you.

NEW MOM: I knew it! You're just not attracted to me anymore. It's the Madonna complex. You just see these—massive—breasts as providing nourishment to your beloved baby.

NEW DAD: (interrupting)…OUR beloved baby.

NEW MOM: And you just can't think of them in a sexual light!

NEW DAD: Well, I wouldn't go that far.

NEW MOM: Oh, sure. I always wanted massive breasts, and now that I've got them, they're leaky!

NEW DAD: (getting turned on) That doesn't bother me.

NEW MOM: Then it's my belly—it's still kind of round.

NEW DAD: No, no—I love your belly. It's very womanly.

NEW MOM: Right, and I suppose I used to look like a boy?

NEW DAD: No, no...

NEW MOM: You just like my belly to match yours so we don't have to lay off the Häagen Dazs.

NEW DAD: No!

NEW MOM: So, it IS my massive breasts!

NEW DAD: No, I love your massive breasts. Believe me, honey, you are so stinking ripe it's killing me!

(He shuts her up with a kiss.)

NEW MOM: (starts again, quietly) You know, some women nurse for years. I could have massive breasts until he's old enough for school. Then I could get pregnant again.

NEW DAD: Whatever you want. I like you both ways. I love you both ways.

NEW MOM: Well, what do YOU want?

NEW DAD: I've changed my mind. Right now, I want YOU. (He caresses her shoulder.)

NEW MOM: Oh. Uh...(stalling; fends him off) Did you hear something?

NEW DAD: I didn't hear anything.

NEW MOM: You sure?

NEW DAD: Positive.

NEW MOM: I think the baby's crying.

NEW DAD: He's not crying. What's wrong? Nervous?

(She nods. He takes her in his arms.)

NEW DAD: We need the music.

NEW MOM: Oh, and honey?

NEW DAD: Yes?

NEW MOM: The roses would be okay, too.

(He laughs. They kiss.)

(Fade to black.)

There is sex after childbirth, but it is not the same. There will be stolen nights of weary passion and hurried mornings of good intentions. You will have less time and energy for it and more emotional need. You will have to adjust to different schedules and desires. The frequency of your amour may be less than the national average. Don't despair—statistics about this are likely to be all lies anyway. Ironically, the time you spend together will be more intimate. You will have less sex and more lovemaking.

Vital Questions

There are certain questions that mothers inevitably find themselves asking. These are the most popular:

Can I call you back?

Do you deliver?

Where's the elevator?

Where's the bathroom?

Do you have highchairs?

Is it machine washable?

When is your next sale?

Why does your six-month size only fit three-month-old babies?

Bonus question:

Do you have infant girls' bathing suits with snaps at the crotch?

Crawling Can Be
Hazardous to Your Health

You'll be standing in the grocery line and some demented woman with an adorable two-year-old trailing her will sigh and tell you to enjoy the time that your baby is a baby. You will look at her independent little look-alike and long to run and play with her.

Right now your baby eats, sleeps, and poops. She cries when you put her down and whenever else she feels like it. She smiles, but it could just be gas. She doesn't really look like anyone you know; in fact, she doesn't even have hair yet. The fact of her mere existence keeps you constantly amazed. You are still tired from her birth, not to mention the seemingly constant nursing. Between taking care of her and the house, you have your hands full. You never get bored, and you never have free time.

But you can set her down, answer the phone, and she will be there when you get back. You can lay her on the bed, get dressed, and she will not have fallen off. You can put her in her bouncer seat while you shower without her crying at the shower door. Your floor-to-ceiling bookshelf still has books in the bottom shelves. You don't have toys strewn all over the floor for her father to trip over when he comes home in the dark.

As you get stronger and used to keeping a twenty-four-hour watch on your baby, she gets to be more mobile, more active, and more of a challenge to keep entertained and out of trouble. You have the house baby-proofed, but she manages to get into everything anyway. Now, too, you never get bored, and you never have free time.

By the time your baby is two, you will see a new mother in line at the grocery store, sigh, and say...

Spoiling and the "N" Word

Is it possible to spoil a newborn? No. They need all the loving and hugging and interaction they can get in order to learn security and self-confidence. Believe me, I've researched this to death. I learned that it's not until babies are about six months old that they learn to connect crying with your company. Always respond to a crying baby—something could be wrong. If there isn't, then she just wants you. Here's where the big decision about letting her cry or not comes in. Like the debated decision over whether or not to schedule the baby's feedings and naps, this choice is yours alone.

The easiest way to stop a four-month-old baby from playing with a dangerous or delicate object is to give her something else. ANYTHING ELSE (that's safe). Babies are easily distracted; take advantage of this distractability. At this age, their attention span is still so short that they won't remember what they were playing with before. They are built with this trait to keep mothers sane for as long as possible.

Once the baby is old enough to understand the sharp tone of "no," make sure you use it appropriately. All healthy babies are intensely curious and love to explore. That's how they learn. If you are a neatnik, bite your tongue—a child's curiosity does not make for a tidy house. Know that if your house is always spotless, something is wrong.

A friend of my husband's came over one afternoon when the baby was busy pulling the books out of our bookshelf. She had conquered the first shelf, gumming the volumes one by one, and was pulling apart the second shelf. The friend looked at me kind of sideways and asked if I ever said "no" to the kid. I told him I wasn't about to waste a good "no" on a bunch of books that could be easily cleaned up. It would be like crying "wolf." I'd save it for when she put a penny in her mouth or when she learns to unlatch the baby latch on the cleaning supply cupboard. This is not to say that I will let her tear apart the toilet paper rolls, but allowing her to check out the books is safe—and time-consuming enough for me to make some phone calls.

When the baby gets older, she will start mimicking you. Be careful. You shake your head enough times, and she'll shake hers too. Eventually, she'll shake her head, anyway. My baby-sitter is a former kindergarten teacher from El Salvador. She comes to my home twice a week while I work. Part of her conversation with my baby used to consist of a lilting "no-no-no" and it is the most hilarious thing to hear my baby say "no-no-no" as she is devouring deli-sliced turkey piece by piece. She doesn't know what it means unless it has a stern tone of voice behind it. Then she cries.

The other aspect of spoiling that mainly concerns the first child is the great number of toys and gifts they are likely to receive. Keep in mind that:

Spoiling has little to do with abundance and a lot to do with attitude.

A child who expects a lot, doesn't share, and acts out regardless of instruction is spoiled, even if she only has three toys. A child who is guided by a firm and consistent hand can be delightful and generous, even if she has fifty toys. It is hard to discipline tiny beings that you love, especially when they cry so easily. But as long as you let them know that, although you love them, bad behavior will not be tolerated, they will be okay.

Be thankful that you have at least six months before you have to worry about it.

Twenty-Four-Hour Leave

How long has it been since you were alone with your husband? I mean really alone, without the baby between you in any sense of the word? No matter what you plan to remedy the situation, be patient. It might not turn out the way you imagine it.

I counted the weeks until my husband and I could go away for a romantic night ALONE. Romance is always lurking when you are full of your love's child and when that child is just born. Nevertheless, the real-life drudgery of motherhood can take its toll.

I scoured the travel books until I found the perfect little hideaway on the beach not too far from four-star restaurants, and not too close to television. My mother drove two hours to come to baby-sit and I spent two days on a written list of do's and don't's (which she totally ignored, of course). I bought a new pair of sexy jeans, as sexy as I could get, since I didn't quite fit into my pre-pregnant pair. After six months, my weight was back to normal, but my body wasn't quite the same. At least my garter belt still fit. I had a manicure, a pedicure, and a haircut. My husband had the car washed and waxed.

We set off, and I couldn't get my mind off the baby. What was she doing? What was she eating? Did she miss us already? What would happen when she woke up at night and we weren't there? Was I going to worry about her the whole time I was gone?

We reached our romantic hotel and found a quiet spot for watching the sunset. I found a pacifier in my purse. I saw baby booties in the clouds. I heard children's laughter in the distance. My husband made toasts to our happiness. We smiled at the potential for uninterrupted romance and, better yet, uninterrupted sleep. Finally, I started to relax.

After a lovely dinner, we returned to our room. I took my time getting all dolled up for an intimate evening. We called home to say goodnight. All was well. We lay down to kiss—and fell asleep.

We slept through the night, a heavy, blissful slumber. I awoke refreshed and ready to go. I was finally enjoying our freedom.

We went outside and had breakfast by the ocean. Jon watched the children playing. I tried to distract him, but it was impossible. We called home. All was well—but not for Jon. HE wasn't having fun anymore—he missed the baby. HE wanted to go home. I couldn't decide if I wanted to kiss him—or hit him.

Maybe we'll try it again sometime. Probably, we'll bring the baby along—and my mother to baby-sit.

The Six O'Clock Scramble

You and the baby and your husband get home late from two different directions. You rush around the kitchen preparing, simultaneously, a nutritious meal for your fussy baby, a quick but hearty meal for your hungry husband, and a quick but labor-intensive salad for yourself. Dividing your conversation between the two members of your family, you tie a bib around your husband's neck. You don't even realize your mistake until he tells you it's too tight. (No wonder the baby hates it!)

At the sound of your baby's name, you snap back to reality. If you are not already crying, you lie down on the floor and laugh until you do.

By and large, mothers and housewives are the only workers who do not have regular time off.

—*Anne Morrow Lindbergh*

YOU KNOW YOU'RE A MEMBER OF CLUB MOM WHEN...

- you start eating bologna sandwiches
- people, including your husband, take your word for it
- even your mother starts listening to you
- the cassettes in your car play songs that rhyme
- a trip to the grocery store takes two hours
- Thanksgiving dinner is at your house
- recycling means eating the baby's leftovers
- you suddenly own a dozen videos, all featuring animals that sing
- you don't mind making love less often than the national average—in fact, you don't believe the national average

KISS IT
GOOD-BYE

Old Friends

Your good friends will want all the glorious details of Junior's coming-out party, if only for curiosity's sake. Spare them the physical facts. They will be more intrigued by your attempts at verbalizing the feeling of awe that new life inspires. After all, the "miracle of birth" is a tired (though absolutely appropriate) term. ("Tired" is an equally appropriate, but not thoroughly understood, concept to the uninitiated.) If you maintain conversations at this esoteric level, your old friends will be apt to stick around longer. This is especially important if they are childless, and even more vital if they are single, because soon you will have ABSOLUTELY NOTHING in common.

"What about the people at work?" you protest. On a relative scale, office news and gossip will be the equivalent of small talk. Even then, with your altered perspective, you'll have to police your conversations in order to remain within the confines of their understanding. No, I am not giving these wonderful women short shrift. They are still wonderful. But your relationship with them will diminish to the point of being a luxury.

Before I was pregnant, I didn't have any friends with children. Now my best friends have children. Unfortunately,

THESE ARE NOT THE SAME FRIENDS. But I can have endless hours of fun and conversation with a mother whose life has nothing in common with mine—except her membership in Club Mom. With nonmothers of similar backgrounds, education, and interests, I am usually tapped out in about twenty minutes. Twenty minutes, during which I furtively keep watch over my daughter while they disdain my rudeness in not maintaining eye contact. Hey, I used to feel the same way! If your friends already have children, you are lucky indeed.

In place of your old friends, you will see a lot more of your family— WHETHER YOU LIKE IT OR NOT. People just love babies, especially when they can give them back to their moms at diaper-changing time. Their fascination with your baby increases exponentially when the child is their blood relation. Some relatives won't get into the swing of things until the baby is past the blob stage and into the little person stage. Others will adore her only UNTIL she starts talking back. Best of all are those who would like nothing more than to clean that cute little tush or soothe a teething infant. Just remember, you are no longer the main attraction at your house and you never will be again. Be grateful: you may get some free baby-sitting out of it.

Satin Sheets

Close your eyes. Relax. Now, what comes to mind when you hear the word "satin"? Romantic interludes with candles and champagne? Steamy sex with black garters and lace? Or just the ultimate luxury in boudoir accoutrements?

Now, let's start over. What do you think of when you hear the word "flannel"? Cold weather gear? Grandma? The Bounty man (as in paper towels)?

Ever since I can remember, I've longed for satin sheets. In novels, passionate nights are never spent on cotton sheets— I don't care what the thread count is. They're always satin. When I was in college I bought imitation satin comforters and satin-like polyester nightgowns to overwhelm my boyfriend. I'm not sure if he noticed, but romance for me was never the same without these niceties. Now that I can afford such luxury, something else always seems to be more important (like diapers, for instance).

Besides, it seems so conniving to buy satin sheets myself. I picture getting them for Valentine's Day, a gift so exciting that mon ami and I must try them out immediately.

I've mentioned this to my husband every January, but he never seems to remember on February 14. Sound familiar?

This year, he brought me the seventy-five dollars that he'd refused to shell out for a dozen roses. I had made the mistake of drilling him earlier that week about unnecessary purchases. (I didn't mean presents for me, of course, but he had impulsively bought me a wonderfully romantic pin with two lovesick coyotes on it the week before, so I didn't really mind.) I was a tiny bit proud that he had paid attention. Satin sheets don't come to HIS mind very often, because he's already slept on some. When he admitted this, he tried to comfort me by explaining that they were no big deal and much too hot in the summer—one of the few practical things he's ever said. And, of course, the baby would stain them with formula the very first morning we brought her into bed to play.

No. My husband has a thing for flannel. Our house was so cold last winter that, by the time I was back from the nursery on my 2:00 A.M. rounds, the sheets were freezing. I bought flannel sheets in self-defense. I must admit, they are soft and warm and wonderful. My husband requested a second set.

You know how it always rains when you forget your umbrella? And when you have it, it never rains? At our house, romance works the same way. If I shave my legs, it will never happen. If I've been so busy that I haven't showered since yesterday morning, sure enough, Prince Charming will get that gleam in his eye. I used to wear sexy teddies under my clothes, but the discomfort of those G-strings are simply not worth the odds. And the satin nightgown I bought for my trousseau gets more action at the dry cleaners. But, when I'm lazily ensconced in a long flannel number, beware.

Maybe it has to do with being subtle, rather than obvious. Some men don't like to be pressured. If you ask me, flannel takes subtlety a little far—like into the neuter zone. I guess that's why flannel gowns always seem to have plenty of flower patterns and industrial strength lace trim.

Now, don't get me wrong, men look great in flannel—it adds a certain rugged, manly air. As for me, I feel sexy when I dress like a bimbo. But I guess my husband doesn't want a bimbo. I guess he wants me.

On second thought, I'll pass on those satin sheets. Flannel can be pretty darn sexy.

Night Owling

I am in the bathtub. It's midnight. You don't believe I am in the bathtub? Okay, you're right. Actually, I meant to write this in the bathtub, but the water splashed up, grabbed my arms, and forced them under until the last of the Big Bird Bath Bubbles had dissolved. I did start with bath oil beads meant for mature adults, but baths just aren't the same without bubbles. I sacrificed my frivolous indulgence in expensive bath accouterments in favor of impulsive shopping for baby clothes. My husband, if he knew (or noticed), would say, "Honey, I want you to be happy. Get yourself some of those luxurious bath bubbles. Don't worry about the money." It sounds good, but I'm the one who pays the bills—what does he know? Anyway, the part about midnight is true.

If you are a night owl, then you know that night owling is not a passing phase. It starts as early in life as your first bedtime. It's not a trait I would like to pass on to my children, considering the high-decibel, time-for-bed-NOW controversies that are inevitable between parent and child. I just like to stay up late. I get my second wind when others start yawning.

The question here, of course, is: why would the mother of an infant be up so late? The obvious answers are that the mother is either a) mentally deficient or b) a glutton for punishment. While not admitting fully to either reason, I can present a case, however warped, for the defense.

Those late hours are important when I don't want it to be tomorrow yet, but I want to recuperate from today. The house is unusually still and the mood is ripe for contemplation. My husband is either with me (as in apart from the baby) or sleeping. This latter state is nice too, because then I don't have to take care of him or clean up after him. So I can be alone—at last. Sometimes, I can even remember what it felt like to be single. Sort of.

Why should I give up this last vestige of freedom when I know that, no matter what time I go to sleep, as soon as I hit that deep, dreamy state, the baby will cry? Less sleep between rounds won't even hit me until sunrise, when the baby's bopping around her crib raring to go. I admit I suffer for this act of self-indulgence. By lunchtime, I'm ready to collapse. By dinner, I vow never to repeat this folly. Then, the moon rises high in the sky, and I do it all over again.

Being a night owl is one of those few things that I am totally in control of. Aside from ice cream and occasional nagging, it's my only vice. I can quit anytime, I swear. Hey, I used to stay up really late and watch old movies. But as a responsible adult, I've cut my prowling back to the pre-midnight hours.

There is one great advantage in being a night owl. I get to experience the absolute depths of frustrated exhaustion when the baby cries in the middle of the night. I mumble under my breath and stare daggers at my husband, who's pretending to sleep. I drag my carcass into the nursery and focus my bleary eyes. And there, like a beacon in the darkness, is the most beautiful little smiling face, covered with real tears, so happy to see me. I melt into utter joy. That one moment awes me with the wonders of mommyhood.

Maybe I'd appreciate it just as much if I were a little more rested…but heck, we only live once, right?

Privacy

There are four kinds of privacy, none of which you will ever have again.

Personal

Personal privacy is the kind you have in the bathroom before the baby is born. At this time you and your husband are purely romantic creatures. You never threaten the vision by shaving your legs in front of him, and he is careful not to use the toilet while you are brushing your teeth. As soon as your water breaks, everything changes. Not only does your husband verify this momentous event for you, he also helps you to the toilet during labor. Once he's cheered the baby's debut, there is no turning back. There is nothing left to hide. You will share the bathroom. After a few months, you may start regressing and close the bathroom door little by little. You won't close it completely, inferring rudely that it's off limits, but you would just as soon have a little privacy. Generally, he will take heed of this nonverbal request. But don't always count on it. The mystery is gone.

Parental

Remember when you used to yell at your mother to stay out of your room? Now, it's Open House. For a good many months, wherever you go, the baby will follow. At first, you will bring the immobile infant along with you. You will store toys in the bathroom so that you can shower for more than thirty seconds without lamenting over your wailing child—the cute one who misses you already. You will learn to relieve yourself with the baby on your lap— anything to keep her smiling. You will hide under the bedcovers when your husband plays with the baby next to you on your day to sleep in. You will have an audience whenever you try on clothes. Just try to get an opinion on anything other than bright prints! You wanted a baby? You've got one.

Public

When you have a baby in your arms, or in your shopping cart, or in a stroller, you are open to the world of baby lovers. This is not so terrible—at least they're not poking your pregnant belly anymore. The rule here is ALWAYS BE NICE. You may need THEM to be nice in a minute when your baby starts to scream.

Partner

Time alone with the new father is at a premium, especially since the two of you may not last much past the time your baby conks out for the night. (Not that the baby will really conk out for the night!) In any case, until the new-baby thrill wears off, everyone you know will want to come play. (The point at which the thrill wears off for visitors is also the point at which you actually begin to have energy for them.) In all the hubbub, be sure to set some time aside for the two of you, even if it means telling Grandma and your husband's old roommate that it's time to go home. While you are throwing them out, remember to invite them for another time, so they don't hate you for life.

Telephone Time

During pregnancy, you and the baby each had a healthy connection to the outside world. Junior had the umbilical cord; you had the telephone. Now, however, the baby is on his own, and so are you. More to the point, the baby now has you to act as his lifeline twenty-four hours a day, while you have...the answering machine.

Here is a sampling of useful messages to help screen your calls, as well as explain to callers why you can't quite make it to the phone right now:

Hi. We can't get to the phone right now, but if you'll leave a message, we'll get back to you...I swear—this time I mean it. BEEP.

Sorry I can't answer this call, but I'm up to my elbows in ...never mind. You don't want to know. Leave a message after the beep. BEEP.

Hello. You've reached the answering machine of the new, improved Blake family. If you really want to talk to us, come see us in person. Viewing hours are from noon to four daily. Donations accepted. BEEP.

Hello. You've reached 451...no, no, don't touch that, honey, thank you...451...no, that's Mommy's...05...stop it, honey...no, please don't touch that. BEEP.

Hi. We're busy with Johnny. One end or the other. We'll have to call you back. BEEP.

Hi. You've reached the Gardner residence. If your call is an emergency or involves potential income, please leave a message. Otherwise, try again. BEEP.

Hi (whispered). The baby's sleeping—finally. If we don't return your call by the end of the week, please try us on Saturday after 8:30 P.M. Sunday's my turn to sleep in. BEEP.

Hi. This is 451-0521. Please leave a message here rather than calling me at work. They're mad enough at me these days. However, if you know of a good au pair, leave the message anywhere you like and say it's urgent. (It is!) BEEP.

Hello, you've reached the Levine family. Sorry we can't come to the phone, but this baby is so cute you won't believe it. He has the softest skin in the world—and the biggest eyes. Leave your number so we can tell you all about him. (I'm beginning to think this machine's broken—no one's left a message all week.) BEEP.

Hi. If this is another insurance salesperson, the answer is still no. BEEP.

At the tone, please leave a message. BURP. No, that wasn't the tone. That was the baby. HERE's the tone—BEEP.

Hi. It's Tuesday. I think it's Tuesday. Anyway, leave a message and we'll get back to you later today...or tomorrow ...or the next day...or the day after that. BEEP.

Hello. We can't get to the phone right now. In fact, we can't find the phone right now. So please leave a message. BEEP.

Hi. Please leave a message at the sound of the beep. If it's you again, Mom, hang up before the beep—you're filling up the machine. BEEP.

Hi. Say hi, Sally. Come on, baby. She said hi just a minute ago, I swear. Come on, Sally, honey, please say hi. Do it for Mommy. You can do it. I know you can. She really CAN say hi. BEEP.

Night Life

Don't worry about missing out on night life. You'll be so tired that you won't even want to spend the time it takes to pull yourself together into that hip, gorgeous creature you used to be.

If you do, you may end up someplace with loud music and a bunch of overdressed singles trying to find what you already have. And you wasted twenty bucks on a baby-sitter!

So, go someplace with a piano bar. It's more conducive to the mood you're looking for. The challenge, of course, is preserving that mood until you get home, dismiss the baby-sitter, check on the baby, and get comfortable. On second thought, maybe you'll have more energy in the morning—before the baby wakes up. If you recognize this as the joke it really is, then you are fortunate to have maintained your sense of humor.

Next time...stay home.

Discussions of
World Peace

Forget about it.

It's dubious if you should continue your newspaper subscription for the first six months of parenthood. Even if your brain isn't Jell-o, reading time just doesn't exist. As for watching TV news two days in a row—unless your baby is on some incredibly regular feeding schedule, don't even dream about this.

When your brain does click back into gear, it will be on automatic pilot. You will recite nursery rhymes you didn't think you knew. You will find yourself singing Raffi's songs to yourself in the shower. If you don't know who Raffi is, don't worry—you will.

Never fear. Current events in history, however exciting, are happening without you. Current events in your house require your every waking moment.

Maybe next year...

YOU KNOW YOU'RE A MEMBER OF CLUB MOM WHEN...

- sweats are your favorite outfit
- silk blouses are a distant memory
- "dressing up" means your best jeans
- 7 A.M. is sleeping in
- you are ready for bed at the same time you used to be dressing for dates
- Miss America contests are no longer a threat—it's easy to be glamorous if you've never had children
- other women no longer consider you a threat
- you forget your own birthday

HAZARDS
FOR NEW
MEMBERS

The Experts

"**W**hen should my baby sit up? Say her first word? Crawl? Get teeth? When should she start on solid food? Stop using a bottle? Feed herself? What are the rules?" I stood in my pediatrician's office demanding answers.

My pediatrician is a grandfather. I would have liked a mother, but there weren't any nearby. I chose this man for his wisdom and his relaxed, comforting attitude. He is cautious when it counts, and he keeps up with the new research. But mostly he has seen it all, and he loves children. He watched my daughter squirm in my arms and answered me patiently.

"Babies don't know the rules," he said. "Provide them with opportunities and they'll get to the next step when they are ready. Rules were made for the benefit of mothers."

"But what about the experts?!" I exclaimed.

"Beware of the experts," he said. "Haven't you noticed that they have all the answers—but they don't always agree?"

He took stock of my look of incredulity and continued. "They all have some good things to say, but many of the popular ones tend to ride the trends. That's why they're popular. Since Americans are in a hurry for everything, we push our children faster and faster."

He admitted that he admires how the Europeans patiently allow their babies to enjoy their bottles until they are good and ready for a cup. He doesn't agree that all infants should feed themselves by twelve months of age. He said that when my baby wants a spoon, let her have it...and not to forget to put on my raincoat.

He said that it's just as normal for a child to get teeth at four months as it is at eight, to walk at nine months or fifteen. He chuckled at my orthodontically correct pacifiers and my concern over rival formula brands. He said it's mothers like me who keep these companies in business. When I told him that I got those brands at the hospital, he explained that hospitals use certain brands because they get them free. Nowadays, he said, most formula products are equally good.

I stared at my feet awhile and cleared my throat. "So, who's the expert? Me?"

He smiled at me and shook his head. He held his finger out and my daughter curled her little hand around it. "She is."

The ideal mother, like
the ideal marriage,
is fiction.

—*Milton R. Saperstein*

Other Kids

Other kids will give your baby colds, the flu, and conjunctivitis. They will affectionately poke her in the eye with their fingers, bang her on the head with their books, and push her away from their Duplos.

They will also give her hugs, raisins, and a broadened outlook on life. They will even wear her out so that she sleeps through the night.

You will learn a lot by watching your baby play with other kids. Your baby won't really play with them, but she'll be happy to play around them. At a children's store, I watched my daughter ignore a two-year-old's attempt to keep a roller coaster toy (with colored wooden beads on shaped wires) to herself. My daughter calmly proceeded to crawl to each place the older girl dragged the toy and play around the girl's possessive embrace. I learned that my daughter is centered in her desires and is secure and confident enough to go after them. For the first time, I saw her as an independent person. Regardless of what you learn when you watch, you will get a kick out of it.

So, watch them play. Watch them CLOSELY!

Other Moms

They will give you advice when you don't want it and opinions that are absurd. They will feed your baby food she's never had before and give you hand-me-downs you are embarrassed to use.

They will also give your baby her favorite toys and diagnose croup in two seconds flat. They will understand when you tell them you can't talk now, and they will lend you the car seats their children have outgrown. They will offer shoulders to lean on when you are frustrated about staying home. They'll be friends you can take walks with, despite your slow stroller. They will pinch-hit for your baby-sitter when she flakes out before your doctor's appointment.

They are the ones who will share your excitement when your baby can finally sit up and your despair at having to justify your twenty-four-hour-a-day job to your hungry husband when he comes home to an empty refrigerator.

You can bring your baby to play in their sandboxes, and they can bring their kids to jump in your pool.

Other mothers will automatically become your friends as soon as you are pregnant. Beware of the ones you wouldn't normally want to have as friends. It will be easy to be friends with the ones who share your laid-back (or uptight) style of mothering, but don't overlook the benefits of being friendly with those who can widen your horizons.

Be generous with other mothers; you will depend on them more often than you think. You will also learn from them. And you will have more fun with them and their children than you could ever have imagined before you joined the Club.

Beware of NOT getting to know other moms.

Your Mother

Who is the most logical person to trust as your baby-sitter? That's right, your mom. After all, she raised you and you turned out okay...didn't you? Just how old are you, anyway? If your baby is her first grandchild—even her first local grandchild—quite a few years may have gone by since your mother last took care of an infant. You can always give her a refresher course on infant and child CPR. You can remind your mom that the baby should sleep on her belly and not on the bed. What you can't do is change some of her antiquated ideas on childrearing. So, beware:

Grandmas love to feed the baby. The first time I left my mom in charge, she had a cupful of ice cream down my three-month-old baby before I had finished dressing! As much as I protested, my mother insisted on feeding the baby oatmeal and strained carrots before the hour was over. She fed me food that early, she said, so what was the harm? I just didn't want the baby to get used to it. Why should I have to hassle with food when she was perfectly happy on formula? All the moms I know have experienced this feeding frenzy with Grandma.

If you are looking the other way, your mom will be the first to have your baby in the stroller, the pool, and the shower. She'll try to avoid diapers, clothing, and the car seat.

Be careful of what you say to her. Otherwise, she'll give you a heart-breaking preview of how it will feel when your baby says that to YOU, years from now.

There is a solution to these potential hazards. Lay down the law about everything you can think of before leaving your baby with Grandma. She won't pay any attention to your speech, but at least you'll feel better. Do remember to be patient with her, especially if she lives within a two-hour drive. She'll be your Number One baby-sitter simply because she loves that little cutie more than anyone else possibly could. Although she may stretch the parameters of your rules, she'll be sure that nothing happens to the baby.

If she starts giving YOU directions on child-rearing, don't get upset about it. You hold the ultimate trump card. In fact, if she starts getting on your nerves about ANYTHING, simply threaten her with baby deprivation. Tell her she can't come see the baby until she lightens up.

Remember, A BABY IS POWER!

Your Mother-in-Law

Oh, my son's my son
'til he gets him a wife,
but my daughter's my daughter
all her life

—*D. Craik*

Has your mother-in-law kept her distance from you and the baby? You may be happy about this now, but you are losing a valuable ally. She had a baby once (at least) and can be a great source of inspiration. She also has every right to love this baby as much as your mother, with all the inherent pros and cons. If she is hanging back a bit, don't take it as an insult. She may be wary of invading your turf. Invite her into the baby's life. She may be able to offer helpful hints and alternative methods you haven't heard about. Not only will this pay off for you in terms of help, but also in appreciation from your husband.

If your mother-in-law is the meddling type, things can be a bit sticky. Be sure to tread lightly lest you touch off a major family feud. There are no prizes in this real-life game. If possible, let your husband handle it. If not, treat her as you would your mother. That is, remember to temper your blunt honesty with respect. Perhaps you could suggest other ways in which she could help you out. Do not simply live with her dominance. You will resent her, and your baby will eventually pick up on this hostility.

The bottom line is this: not everyone has a grandma, let alone two. Let your baby be blessed with lots of loving relatives.

The Kitchen

Do you love your kitchen? In all of the books on child rearing I've read, the experts always tell you how to manage the baby while in the kitchen. Use a baby carrier, they say, or a baby seat while you're cooking. They insist that babies love to play with pots and pans while you are in the kitchen. I find this all quite insulting—that they would assume a modern woman such as I would actually spend a lot of time in the kitchen. I don't know about you, but I HATE THE KITCHEN!

The absolute worst part about being a new mother is that, somehow, I find myself in the kitchen as much as those experts said I'd be. YUCK! Since I am home with the baby, I am the one who ends up cooking, cleaning, and preparing meals for all of us at different times. As much as I looked forward to having a dishwasher, I hate having to fill it and empty it every day. I don't like to cook, but I do like to eat, so here we are.

Never underestimate the value of points. All time spent in the kitchen is worth points. Fixing my husband's dinner nets about ten good points. Fixing dinner for company is worth about fifty points, especially if you (and the baby) get stuck in the kitchen alone for any amount of time. In the winter, my husband always cooks for company—everybody hangs out in the kitchen and he gets a lot of points. These points are from the company, who mistakenly assume that he does this all the time. (This would be impractical, since he doesn't get home from work until at least eight o'clock.) It's irrelevant anyway, because other people's points don't go in my book. But when it's nice outside, and he entertains while I cook, then I figure I earn at least 100 points. He's the first to agree. These points are applicable to anything I want: sleeping in, extra baby-sitting days, a new dress. Granted, with good timing and credit cards, I can usually manage these anyway. On the point system, I really feel that I've earned them. I'm working on a new car.

After long and hard research on how to avoid spending a great part of your day in the kitchen, I have only one thing to say: Domino's.

Baby-Sitters

Your mother or father might exhaust your baby with so much attention. Your brother might forget about her in the ninth inning when the bases are loaded. Your sister might bore her with a fashion magazine. A professional baby-sitter might be just the answer.

A qualified baby-sitter loves children and is trustworthy. Don't be embarrassed to check out a baby-sitter's references. Your baby's life hangs in the balance. It is vital that she knows all the medical and safety procedures in case of an emergency. If she doesn't, and you like her anyway, sign her up for a class at the local Red Cross. Most chapters offer infant and child CPR and First Aid (often in Spanish as well as in English). They are also the best referral source for other courses available in your area.

Trust your instincts. Just because someone else likes a particular baby-sitter doesn't mean you have to. You should be comfortable giving directions to her, and you should hang around enough to watch her in action. If you'd like her to clean up after the baby and wash her clothes, make sure this is not a problem with her. Find out if she has raised children of her own. If she has and they are in jail, perhaps she is not the one for you. Find out how this job fits in with her goals. If baby-sitting is an interim job for her, it's best if her main interest is in a child-related field, like teaching.

Don't trust someone just because she comes through a reputable agency. She still may fall asleep in front of the television—with your baby in her arms. One woman who was sent to us through an agency—on a day when I was too sick to care for my ten-week-old baby—was a naturalist. I was happy to have her point out that I shouldn't use foil under my burners due to the toxins released, but I was not so thrilled when she was reluctant to give the baby prescription medicine.

Another woman I employed once a week for several months was really good. She told me right off that she was a Jehovah's Witness and I told her it was fine as long as she kept her religion to herself. Things were fine when I was working at home. The day I had to go to a meeting, I gave her my paranoid instructions for an emergency and found out that, for religious reasons, she didn't believe in blood transfusions. Despite the risks, I wanted my baby to have a transfusion if she needed it, and I worried all day. My sitter said she'd follow my wishes, but her reluctance was apparent.

Also beware of anyone who might have a dangerous ex-husband or a son involved with drugs. It took a long time to make this baby. Don't let anyone harm her.

My favorite baby-sitters, aside from neighborhood moms who trade off in a pinch, are people who have been employed by someone I know for a long time. If they aren't available, maybe they have relatives who are equally responsible.

You still have to LIKE a baby-sitter. Better yet, THE BABY HAS TO LIKE HER.

When you're out and a sitter is in charge, don't feel silly calling home a lot. The sitter will know you care, and you will be more at ease. Be sure to start looking for sitters well before you need them—just as you'd do if you were exploring day care.

When it comes to sitters: use caution—and common sense.

Birthday Parties

Now that you are entering the world of babies, you are sure to be invited to a lot of children's birthday parties. It is amazing how many parents have big wingdings for their child's first birthday. I have seen clowns, ponies, and magicians. These will be great entertainment in a few years, but let's get real. These parties are for the parents. According to child development theories, the general rule of thumb for the number of children at a birthday party is double the child's age.

Believe it or not, birthday parties can get very political very quickly. I have a neighbor, Jane, who doesn't particularly like another neighbor named Anne. This, of course, is her divine right. Anne invited Jane's children to her child's big birthday party. When it came time for Jane's child's birthday several months later, she decided to just have a small party and didn't invite Anne's children. She figured that they never played together anyway, so what was the big deal? To Anne, it was a very big deal. At a mutual friend's party, Anne dragged her children away from Jane's without so much as a hello. Now Jane feels bad. Should she have invited her?

Do whatever makes you happy about your child's birthday party. But beware of social complications!

The Three R's

At least one great conductor attributes his genius to hearing his mom's favorite symphonies in utero. If you must have Junior in the college prep day care center, then go ahead, sign him up. Just remember, there are a lot more important things to be learned before reading, writing, and arithmetic.

In the book *Dibs: In Search of Self* by Dr. Virginia Axline, a little boy, who turned out to be quite brilliant, was initially thought to be retarded due to his lack of interaction with the world. His well-meaning parents had educated him so early and so emphatically that he never knew he was loved merely for BEING. Rather, he was valued for DOING. His total withdrawal was a form of unconscious rebellion. This is an extreme case, but a good example of the possible consequences of replacing bonding with early education. Dr. Axline, who developed Play Therapy, was able to help the boy get back in touch with his own identity by providing him with a generic playroom, where he felt comfortable to play freely. Eventually, his activities revealed the source of his problems and allowed him to resolve the conflicts.

Many child development specialists believe that just because a child has the potential to learn certain skills doesn't mean he has to learn them all NOW. Kids grow up too fast as it is. And just because infant math lessons exist doesn't mean you have to buy them. People invent products all the time, hoping to create a need. Just look at feminine hygiene deodorants…

Let the buyer beware.

College Savings Plans

Financial institutions have
seen the future—and it is US. We have unknowingly created a
new niche of investors. New parents, whether they have
money or not, want the best possible future for Junior. We are
constantly bombarded with investment strategies for the
college years.

By now, you may have seen the complicated formulae
they use to estimate the exorbitant price of higher education
in the year 2010. They start with the number of years you
have to save, then figure in the probable rate of inflation. The
projected costs are astronomical. Some states have investment programs for state colleges, but that can be a gamble.
Either a headstrong child or the future quality—and
solvency—of that institution (or both) could alter your plans.
All the suggested strategies have you saving and (ideally for
them) investing several hundred dollars a month.

But HOLD ON HERE! While these plans are all viable
and prudent, most of us are still reeling from the burden of
diapers and formula on our current budgets. A child brings a
lot of hidden expenses beyond a crib and lots of little clothes
and shoes. This is the time most families invest in life
insurance, bolster their health care plans, fence in the yard,

and look into some form of day care. Many families trade dreams of a new car for the advantages of a full-time mother. Next we plan for a sibling—and a bigger house. All of the expected and unexpected expenses of parenthood combine to offer us a mighty challenge: how to maintain a level of lifestyle similar to the one we had previously. It's an old saying, but let's say it again:

Don't throw the baby out with the bath water.

Although planning for your baby's education is very important, most experts advise that your baby's comfort and happiness throughout her childhood should take first priority. Don't go back to work early just to save for her college fund. She'll appreciate you more now. This is also the ideal time to help her build the confidence she'll need later—especially if she DOES have to pay her own way.

Likewise, don't scrimp on medical care, food, or even toys. Toys are how children learn. Without them, she may never even make it to college! If you come across an extra big tax return, or win the lottery, by all means put aside a chunk of it for your alma mater. Invest the baby's birthday, Christmas, and Chanukah money for the same purpose. But don't take too much away from now to provide for later.

People seem to work harder when they have someone they love to provide for—so chances are good you'll make more money as time goes on. And who knows…maybe she'll get a scholarship.

Playing Favorites

Suddenly, everyone is an expert. Especially men. An old family friend sat me down before my baby was born and insisted that I face the fact that everything in my relationship with my husband was about to change. This happy family man told me that along with his first child came the most difficult period of adjustment he and his wife ever had.

Even my hairdresser, an open homosexual who really does trim only half an inch when I ask for half an inch, got serious with me recently. He hears a lot of clients bemoan their relationships because a new baby has come between the parents. He even wanted to know if I had considered an affair, because I reminded him of Hope on "thirtysomething." (Don't you hate how everyone says that, just because you are a mother? I hope I don't snivel that much!) I assured him that I would love to have an affair—with my husband. If only I had that much energy...

Evidently there is some plague going around that causes mothers to focus all their attention on the babies. Granted, survival of the fittest mandates a great deal of this preoccupation with the weakest, but it should not be all that lopsided. You hope that your husband is as overjoyed and involved as you are in the baby experience. If not, encourage him. The baby is equally his domain. If you two don't share now, there's likely to be intense competition for the child's affection later.

Your man should be Number One all the time. This will be easy, since watching him grow into fatherhood is sure to make you fall in love with him all over again—and for even better reasons. Just watch how gently he wipes the baby's runny nose. And you are Number One to him, as well. After all, he'd be just another lonely bachelor without you. This way, the baby can revel in the abounding household love and be ungrudgingly loved by all. Our baby smiles the brightest when she sees us kissing. Don't go so far as to play games like "who would save whom first."

Save the relationship first!

A man likes to believe he is King. My husband wanted to eat Thanksgiving dinner on his April birthday. Whatever you want, I told him, as I watched him feed the baby. He acknowledged that it's nice to be King. I encouraged him, "That's right, you can do whatever you want." We looked at each other and laughed, with the unspoken "within limits" hanging between us. Husbands work hard. They miss out on a lot of the fun with the baby. Love them up. Having children is joyous—especially when it's shared.

YOU KNOW YOU'RE A MEMBER
OF CLUB MOM WHEN...

- you've forgotten the name of your manicurist
- you start calling everyone "honey"
- you have more fun in a toy store than a boutique
- your dry cleaning bills go down while all the others go up
- you drive five miles out of your way for double coupons
- your topics of conversation can bore the patience out of an old friend
- your favorite TV star is Cookie Monster
- you have more real friends at the park than at the office

MEMBERSHIP
MYTHS

Nap When the Baby Naps

This is the biggest joke any new mother knows. New babies cannot entertain themselves. It takes them a while to be able to hold their heads up, let alone hold rattles. They pretty much just LOOK. At first they can't see much past your face. It logically follows that you are the best show in town. Since you haven't yet got the hang of laundering—or the desire to launder—those milk-stained sheets with your one free hand, you've got plenty to do when the baby's napping. Returning phone calls has to be done now as well. Nonsleeping babies of any age will cry until they get your undivided attention—and you get a hang-up on the other end of the phone. Forget about reading the paper, or even your favorite child-care magazines. Nap time is your only chance to read the mail. Oh, did I mention breakfast? Your time is so consumed by the baby that you'll be lucky to eat at all. And you NEED to eat. My motto was: breakfast by 2 P.M.

So, now you've eaten breakfast, read the mail, returned the most important phone calls, and you are just lying down on the bed. Wait...what was that noise? Baby, of course. Time to get up.

All Babies Are Beautiful

All babies are NOT beautiful. YOUR baby is always beautiful, but that doesn't necessarily hold true for your neighbor's kid.

Many black babies are beautiful because their skin is like creamy mocha. Many oriental babies are beautiful because their eyes and usually thick, dark hair give them character. Please, don't anyone take offense. But most other babies start out looking like E.T.

How can you tell the mother of a baby who looks older than his grandpa that he's beautiful? You don't have to. Say he's quite a boy, or that he has a lot of personality. As long as you are smiling while you say it, she will take it as a compliment.

My baby is no exception. I thought she was beautiful from the start. Everyone else agreed—even the doctor, who's seen plenty of babies. She certainly is beautiful now. But when I look back at some of those first pictures, I have to wonder.

(Did I hear somebody say, "Phone home"?)

Every beetle is a gazelle in the eyes
of its mother.

—*Moorish proverb*

Grandmas Bake Cookies

My mother didn't even make cookies for my school bake sales. If work didn't leave her time to slice-and-bake, she picked some up at the bakery. If your mother isn't the apron type, don't expect her to start baking now that she's a grandma. She won't.

When I came home from the hospital, I expected my mom to take over. She did, but not the housework. She took over the baby. I had to tear the baby out of my mother's arms just to feed her. As a joke, we called her the Grandma from Hell. As long as she was around, no one else had a chance.

At least she wasn't like MY grandma, who didn't like kids at all. She did make me fresh orange juice once, but then we got into an argument about pollution and we didn't really talk again until I could legally join her for cocktails.

If your baby's grandma bakes cookies for you, count your blessings. Then send her over.

A Baby's Place Is
in the Home

Notice how you rarely see babies on television? Dixie Martin is a featured character in "All My Children," yet, since her much heralded baby was born, we've only seen him about once a month. We are to assume that he is always upstairs sleeping. Now, it's true that babies are allowed on the set for only a short time. Usually twins are used, so they can spell each other. Actually, TV producers prefer to avoid the planning and expense of babies altogether. But somebody ought to tell the writers that, while Dixie professes to be a concerned mother, she ought to be arrested for child abandonment! That baby must be well over a year old now, and he still sleeps all the time! Oh, she takes him out for viewing on special occasions, but she NEVER takes him out of the house.

Soap opera characters often have the luxury of having a nurse watch the baby while the mother goes about her business. Even if you have this advantage, you and your baby may both be missing out. Babies must learn about their environment sometime, and the sooner they do, the more at ease they will feel. They'll also be better behaved by the time they can really make a fuss. You can have a lot of fun out and about with your baby. I admit that, on a quick flurry of errands, getting your bundle of joy in and out of a car seat is no picnic. But seeing the baby's reaction to stimulation other than the mobile over her crib can be pretty exciting.

Think of your baby as your little pal. As he grows up, with any luck, he will be. Take him everywhere. Babies are incredibly portable. Mine loves clothes shopping with me. She loves the colors of clothes on the racks above her stroller and she's crazy about the three-way mirrors in the dressing rooms. An added bonus is that she usually needs a new diaper by the time I am ready to buy something—so just having her along means I shop without spending any money! When the baby starts crawling, visits to the outside world are a bit more challenging. Then, you can have a great time in the park or visiting other moms with little kids. So, keep your baby bag packed and ready.

You hear me, Dixie?

Having It All

My younger sister is one of those people who is always in the right place at the right time. Wherever she goes, TV news follows. When she waited in line eight hours for *The Phantom of the Opera* tickets, guess who was interviewed? When she ran in the L.A. Marathon as an Achilles Club escort for a handicapped foreign athlete, guess who was interviewed? When an earthquake hit the Los Angeles basin, guess who was interviewed?

Sometimes it seems like if you want to see her, just turn on the news. In fact, she was such a good subject that she recently got her master's degree in broadcast journalism and is now a CBS anchor. While she was in school, she worked for one of the visiting professors, Betty Friedan. After a public seminar on women's roles, guess who was interviewed on the news? You guessed it. I'll never forget what she said:

> **"I want a career and a husband
> and a family.
> I want it all—and I don't want to
> have to choose."**

An optimistic and naive proclamation from an optimistic and naive young woman. Although the women's liberation movement led us down the glory path to equality, the result wasn't about having it all. It wasn't even about paving the way to having it all. No. It was about freedom and opportunity. It was about having CHOICES.

Choice is not a bad thing. It is just not everything. A woman, supernatural in power as she may be, is still only one human being with twenty-four hours every day. She cannot devote all her time to everything. The best part about choice is that we can follow our hearts or our egos, whichever is stronger. For mothers of little babies and young children not yet in school, this choice is a heavy one. The decision will be laced with anxiety. Our generation of women was raised to have successful careers. Whoever thought about how to fit a family into that demanding agenda? So, now, it is a matter of choice.

Fortunately, nothing lasts forever. We can stay home full-time or we can work full-time. We can stay home while the kids are young and work once they are in school. We can stay home when they are babies, work part-time when they are toddlers, and work full-time when they are older. Or, we can work part-time from the start. Now, if only society would come full circle and support stay-at-home mothers as equally as career mothers. Then these choices would really be wide open...and our CHILDREN could have it all.

Many careers are difficult to jump in and out of, especially for younger women who have not yet gotten a foothold in the rat race. Never fear. The rats will always be racing. They are not racing to any particular place, anyway. You have a lifetime to jump back in.

Life is not a sprint: it's a journey of endurance.

The best way to get from start to finish is not necessarily a straight line. Many times, a refreshing break to enjoy life with your baby can be the perfect inspiration for making your work count for more later on.

Once the children are safely in school, a woman can divide her time more easily between her family and her career. When you have a baby and are working by choice, you are trying to have the best of both worlds. But you are not having it all. THERE IS NO SUCH THING!

Quality Time

This is a silly concept that creates anxiety in all mothers. It is supposed to mean that a mother who only spends two hours a day with her baby can have just as rich a relationship—if those two hours are spent playing—as a full-time mother who has to spend a lot of her day busy with housework and other activities. Quality time is often misinterpreted as meaning that, if you can give the baby two good hours, you're off the hook...and that only playtime counts.

My daughter is not yet capable of speaking, but I am sure that if she were, she would assure me that she enjoys having me there to feed her and change her diaper as much as she enjoys our games of peek-a-boo. Okay, she probably likes playing peek-a-boo best, but it's the game, not me. Then again, she likes sitting in a nice clean diaper, too. She'd rather be naked, but now I am straying from the point.

I really believe that ALL the time you spend with your baby is quality time. "With your baby" is the operative phrase here. Ignoring the baby while you dress is not being "with your baby." But talking to the baby while you dress is. Driving your car with her buckled up in the back seat might not be an ideal way to spend your time together, but if you are singing to her and talking about her toys or the fire trucks zooming by, this rates as decent interaction. I daresay that grocery shopping is just as stimulating for infants as playing in the sandbox. Babies love to see the bright colors and shapes of groceries. They love seeing other people. Best of all, they adore seeing the other babies, and there are invariably plenty of babies at the market. Interaction is the key.

The concept of quality time is a logical outgrowth of our fax-obsessed society—there is never enough time. Did anybody else notice that the advent of faxes and fast food forces us to squeeze in more work—rather than allowing us more play?

Let's not make fast parenting as much a part of our lifestyle as fast food.

It is unfortunate that our can't-win society is so quick to point fingers at "bad" mothers who choose to work full-time, while at the same time refusing stay-at-home mothers the respect that would help influence more women to stay at home and enjoy being with their children (as long as family finances permit).

In my opinion, ALL mothers are full-time mothers, some just aren't always there. When they are there, it's ALWAYS quality time.

Children Should Be Seen and Not Heard

This rule should have gone out with the Victorian age. If your baby is more than a few months old and is absolutely quiet at all times, see a doctor. Happy children have a lot to talk about—whether or not we understand their language. There is a huge difference between their sad noises and their happy noises. Babies voices are so pure and beautiful. The sounds they make are hints of their personality. You may get some dirty looks while your baby tests out her vocal chords at the grocery stores, but think of the looks you'd get if you tried to stop her.

For the first few months, your baby will be relatively quiet—aside from crying. She will be so nonverbal, in fact, that you can safely take her to a movie matinee. My baby saw a hokey thriller when she was a few weeks old. She didn't actually SEE it; she alternated between nursing and sleeping. The movie theater was dark, but it was noisy. I held my hands over her little ears for the whole time and my back was killing me by the time it ended. But it was worth it just to get out of the house.

Several months later, I took her to see a romantic comedy. She was much more alert by then, and the endless dialogue moved her to join right in. Obviously she felt her conversation was more interesting than the characters' on the screen. Thrilled at her responsiveness, I was inclined to agree. When we escaped to the quiet lobby, she clammed up. We returned to the movie, and she picked up where she left off. This was determined babbling. This was also our last movie together.

Babies are moody, emotional little creatures. They can cry in a second—and they can stop just as quickly. You will learn to recognize the difference between crying and bawling. Crying is an outburst of frustration that can be remedied by distraction or relief of whatever is ailing them. Bawling is a red-faced ferocity that requires soothing.

This is not to say that a child's natural volume is always appropriate. Be practical—and patient. If you want sushi for lunch, take the baby with you. Give her some steamed rice and toys, and call her attention to the sushi maker. If she cries when the rice sticks to her hands, wipe them off and give her something else. If she cries again for more than a minute, take stock of when she had her last nap. Get your food wrapped up to go, and take her home. Today was just not her day.

The sooner babies learn about the world, the better behaved they'll be in it. So don't be upset when your baby starts talking to the grapefruit. (At least not until she starts demanding answers.)

Traveling Light

These two words comprise one of motherhood's biggest jokes. On the brighter side, you can store your dumbbells in your attic (if you have one), in the box marked "bikinis." Who needs weights when you get your upper body workout by hauling Baby around and hoisting all the attendant necessities? Who needs to pay health club dues for killer exercise sessions when airfare (for traveling with baby) gives you the same results?

There is no need to forego all thoughts of travel because you have a young child. Your relatives will love seeing your baby, and you may even get a chance to go to the bathroom alone. Traveling is no longer simple, however, so plan accordingly.

From here on out, you will be laden with a child, who, unless you want her crawling around O'Hare International, will be in your arms. You will also have a baby bag crammed with as many toys (if you're smart) and diapers (if you're practical) as possible. Don't forget extra baby clothes. The only time I skipped this, my baby started cutting a tooth on the way to the airport and drooled so much she was soaked for the next eight hours. I had to keep stuffing her top with kleenex. I hope she doesn't remember this when she's fourteen and flat-chested. It is also smart to bring medicines for sudden teething episodes and colds.

Don't even bother to bring your favorite fashion or literary magazine—you won't have the room or the time. If you are traveling with a newborn, you will be busy feeding and burping. If you are traveling with an infant, you will be busy entertaining. If you are traveling with a toddler, God help you. A lone tube of lip gloss will be your only comfort.

A word about your husband: if possible, don't leave home without him.

The airlines will not give you a break just because you're traveling with a small infant. Your plane will still miss its connection, even if it's billed as a direct flight that retains its flight number, but changes "equipment" in St. Louis. You will still have to battle long lines at the service desk to book another flight and wait three hours for the next departure. Friendly strangers who have children will smile and play with your baby, but they won't offer to help you. They will move clear across the waiting area as soon as Junior starts to cry.

Before the trip, try to adjust your baby's bedtime little by little towards the time zone you will be visiting. This is much more difficult on the return home, so plan on several days of adjustment without social obligations for either of you. There is a strong probability that your baby will get sick, at least with a minor cold, from the change in time and weather, so be patient. You will probably catch it too.

Make a trip to the toy store before you leave. It is a good idea to pack your baby bag with an assortment of SMALL toys your baby hasn't seen before. Add some borrowed toys from a willing neighbor. The combination of new and borrowed toys saves on the pocketbook without allowing your baby to become attached to a bunch of borrowed toys she may never see again. Don't forget a few old favorites that will make her feel comfortable.

Be sure your baby is nursing on take-off and landing. It can be you, a bottle, or a pacifier. Keep the chewing gum for yourself. Sucking will keep the baby from screaming at the change of air pressure. The inner ear is very sensitive at this stage of life, so take heed. This works.

On a recent trip, I tried to take my baby's car seat with me on the plane without buying an extra ticket. It worked fine on the first flight, a huge jet with lots of empty seats. On the second flight, a smaller plane that was nearly full, I got past the gate, but the stewardess made me check the car seat because it wouldn't fit in the overhead compartment. This actually saved me from paying to check it ahead of time as additional baggage and guaranteed that it got on my plane and would be there for the drive from the airport. I strapped on my baby carrier, and felt safe with my baby in it (despite her protests) whenever the seat belt sign was on. So, if you can't afford another seat for your baby, play dumb and bring the car seat. (Remember, you didn't hear this from me.) The down side is that, if this strategy works, you will have to carry the seat, your baby, and your baby bag through the airport—not a lightweight adventure. Either way, DON'T FORGET YOUR BABY CARRIER.

Avoid the hassle by planning ahead. Be ready for every possible situation. Pack carefully.

There is no such thing as traveling light.

YOU KNOW YOU'RE A MEMBER OF CLUB MOM WHEN...

- spring cleaning takes all summer
- laundry becomes a permanent state of activity
- you thank God, regularly and out loud, for the dishwasher
- you start reading minds
- a lisp is no longer a speech impediment (especially in an adorable child)
- your definition of a "real man" is Mr. Rogers
- you can't remember the last time you read a book without pictures
- there's more sand in your car than at Malibu Beach

CAREER
WOMAN
BLUES

They Used to Call Them Old Maids

L ast week I went to the bank (okay, *we* went to the bank) looking like the epitome of harried motherhood. I had on a dirty T-shirt and leggings. My hair was in a quick (rather than fashionable) ponytail, and my face was devoid of make-up. Come to think of it, I'm not sure I had even washed my face. Thank goodness for automatic tellers—now neither you nor the teller has to see anybody up close.

As I (we) walked back to the car, a woman my age pulled up in a sparkling convertible BMW. She had long brown hair like mine (hers was brushed) and she was wearing a black-checked blazer over a white silk T-shirt and a black linen skirt. She wore sheer dark hose and beautiful high-heeled shoes. Just what *I* would wear if *I* were the unmarried career type or the married without children career type. I knew that if she dropped her checkbook I would find entries for Ann Taylor, Neiman Marcus, and Charles Jourdan. I would find the Elite Sports Club and a French beauty salon. I would find four-star restaurants and TWA. It dawned on me that I was staring at my alter ego.

If she had picked up my checkbook she would have found Toys 'Я'Us™ and pediatricians, discount clothing stores, and auto repair shops, video rental outlets, and grocery stores. Even if I had an excuse to dress the way she did, and had the spare cash for an expensive car, I would certainly no longer have well-manicured hands, perfect accessories, and that cool, assured air of the career woman.

I would still go home to a messy house and try not to trip over the toys. I would still have to make dinner. I would have to keep my child entertained with the open kitchen cabinets while making sure the baby-proof latches worked on the cabinets she wanted open. I would wonder if my husband would be home in time to eat dinner hot. I would make sure not to look in the mirror when I had a chance to go to the john. I would comfort the baby when her new tooth made her cry.

My alter ego would pick up Chinese food and go home to her message machine. The guy she wanted to go out with had finally asked her for a night when she was busy. Her mother had called and has a man in mind for her. A neighbor wants to take her sailing. Her place is spotless. She sits down to scour a new catalog and watches whatever channel she wants on TV. She sees a diaper commercial and laughs at the baby. She calls a girlfriend to go to a movie. She gets her coat and turns off the TV.

My husband once kiddingly said that he saved me from being an old maid. Sometimes I wonder if it would be so bad. Then he comes home. He puts his arms around us for a great big three-way hug. The baby giggles. I stop wondering.

The merest grin of maternal
beatitude
is worth a world of dull virginity.

—*Gerald Gould*

R-E-S-P-E-C-T

My husband and I bought a new car last month. When I signed the loan documents, the salesman asked for my occupation. Since my baby halted my time-consuming career, I have spent all my free time—that is, the time I made free—writing. But it's not like I get a check every week. In fact, most of my time is spent with my baby. The man chuckled and wrote "domestic engineer." I am still insulted. Why is being a mother so inglorious that they have to invent a fancy term for it?

Jon tries to console me by encouraging me to use the word "homemaker." To him, the ultimate job is to create a warm, nurturing environment, a safe haven that is a home. But even empty houses are called "homes" these days—in order to sell better. "Mother" is almost a dirty word. And I can't help thinking of Mrs. Cleaver in her apron and pearls.

So, I keep saying "writer" when anyone asks what I do—and then cringing at the half-truth. I have to work in order to assuage my wounded ego. I have to write because that is what I love to do. But often, when I relax with my neighbor, a true full-time mom, I wonder why I get so anxious after three or four blissful days with my baby. Those days I have with my baby—most of my days—are by far the most joyous and fulfilling. Hey, she took her first steps last week—to me!

But there is still this one tiny part of my brain that was carefully groomed, all my life, to ACHIEVE. And, with all the babies born every day all over the world, motherhood doesn't seem like any big deal.

A dinner guest last night assured me that raising a happy, healthy child IS an achievement, because dysfunction is the norm these days. While this may be a sad-but-true commentary on the state of humanity, it still doesn't satisfy the baby boomer's need for outside recognition.

It all comes down to respect. It is undeniably true that, if all babies had good parenting, a lot of grown-ups would have less problems. If mothers got more respect, they could relax and concentrate on what is really important: human life. Unfortunately, human life just doesn't merit much respect these days. Money does. People often think that money will bring a better quality of life, which in turn will bring a better life. But if we are all busy trying to make the money, what kind of life is it?

The bottom line is that we have to respect ourselves. We must make choices and learn to be comfortable with them. Once we feel good about who we are, others will respect us as individuals. Then someday, maybe, women will have respect without having to work so hard to earn it. The priority for a mother is to be proud of how she handles motherhood, so that her children grow up equally proud.

We are role models.

Domestic engineer, indeed!

But What Do You Do All Day?

Have you wondered about your friends who have small children? In just a few months, you'll learn the answer for yourself. If you are curious, read on.

When the baby was four weeks old, my father called. Up until her birth, our conversations revolved around exercise, diet, and work. This time, I didn't have a lot to offer on these topics, so the conversation died a quick death. He asked if I was bored. No, "bored" definitely did not describe my state of mind. Then he blundered into no man's land and asked the one question that he would forever regret. What do I do all day?

First I asked him what he meant by "day." Did it start with the 2:00 A.M. feeding or the half-hour feeding during sunrise? Did it start when my husband got up for work or when I was finally dressed around 11:00? He said he meant when I was out of bed for good in the morning. I said okay.

At 6:30, I feed the baby, praying that she'll fall back to sleep. No such luck. Change her diaper. She pees mid-change. I change the diaper again and put clothes on her. She spits up. I change her clothes again. By now it's 7:30. We walk to the street for the paper and bring it inside. I put the

189

baby down to make myself some juice. She cries and I pick her up. I make juice with one hand. She squirms, and I drop the juice. I put her down and let her cry while I hurry to clean it up. The phone rings. It's my mother. The doorbell rings, and I scoop up the baby to get it. It's the UPS man delivering a package for next door. I remember my mother, who by now has hung up. I call her back and tell her I can't talk. I sit down with the baby for a minute to show her a rattle. She can hold it, but I'm not sure if she really cares about it or if it's a grasping reflex.

I remember to call the doctor to schedule an appointment. I dial the phone, and the baby starts crying. I look at the clock and realize it's 8:30 and she's hungry again. The doctor isn't in yet, anyway. I feed the baby, and change the diaper. Thank goodness for the musical mobile. I get inspired and try a new outfit on the baby. Already too small...damn. I call the doctor, schedule an appointment. I realize what day it is and make a mental note to pay some bills. I also want to make some calls about life insurance. I bring the baby and her seat to the bathroom. I wash my face. The phone rings—wrong number. The baby is asleep. Yay! I put her in the crib and sit at the desk to pay bills. I remember my juice and go get it. I take a sip and remember we need groceries. I make a list. I write a few checks and find that I'm out of stamps. I put a load in the washing machine. The baby wakes up. My husband calls to see how it's going. He forgot a phone number. I pick up the baby. She stinks. We return to the changing table. I change her and pack her bag for errands. It's only 10:00 A.M.

Get the picture? As the baby gets older, you are just as busy in other ways— entertaining her, keeping her out of trouble. As wonderful and amazing as she is when she first exists, she quickly learns new skills that keep you constantly engrossed. It's a lot of work...and a lot of fun.

But if anyone ever asks what you do all day, MAKE SOMETHING UP!

A baby is an inestimable blessing
and bother.

—*Mark Twain*

Ego, Ergo, I Go

If you have to work to provide food and shelter for your child, be proud of your efforts. This is an accomplishment. If you don't have to go back to work, but you really want to, by all means do it. At this early stage in your Club membership, love and security are the vital components of child-rearing. A good caregiver can offer these. This is not to say that you should spend all the baby's waking hours at the office. Why have a baby at all if work is your absolute priority? Nevertheless, if you will be happier doing productive work outside the home, you will be happier when you are home.

Your baby has an astounding awareness. She takes her cues from you. If you will be a happier mom, she will be a happier baby.

Working at Home

This is the ideal situation. It takes concentration, persistence, and an empty refrigerator. Good luck!

YOU KNOW YOU'RE A MEMBER OF CLUB MOM WHEN...

- "vacation" no longer applies to you
- you can say no and mean it
- you can translate babyspeak
- it's 3 P.M. and you haven't brushed your hair yet
- you unplug the phone—and don't miss it
- you finally learn how to cook
- you start shopping by catalog
- you blow the money you've been saving for that slinky red dress on a fuzzy little snowsuit with bunny ears
- Raffi replaces the Rolling Stones on your hit parade
- you smile at squalling babies in department stores

PAST THE PLEDGE STAGE: PLANNING FOR NUMBER TWO

Once More—with Feeling

Why is it that as soon as a baby is a year old and you finally feel confident about the whole thing, those maternal urges start all over? Here are some possibilities:

- You have a short memory.
- You miss the baby-ness of your baby.
- You want to try it again now that you know what NOT to do.
- You think the new maternity clothes look pretty cute.
- Your baby's outgrown rompers are too adorable to sit in a box in the garage.
- You need a new excuse to pig out.
- You don't want your baby to miss having a playmate.
- You are finally getting along with your sister and want your baby to have the same opportunity twenty or thirty years from now.
- You think the baby is bound to look like you this time.
- It's your turn to name the baby, and you've got a good one picked out.
- You've given up on your career anyway.

- You've managed to maintain a hold on your life's work and you figure "what the hell?"
- The "experts" say that a two-and-a-half-year difference is the easiest for you and the best for the baby.
- You want five more babies, so you figure you'd better get going.
- You are insane.

Whatever your reason might be, look back in that baby book and try to recall what it really felt like to be a nursing zombie. Try to remember how delightful your pregnancy was. Try to balance your checkbook!

If all you can think of is that awestruck moment when your baby was born...and the joy the baby has given you... and the love that has overwhelmed your family...and you're really, truly ready...

GO FOR IT!

SEMEL MATER   SEMPER MATER

Welcome to
CLUB MOM

ONCE A MOTHER, ALWAYS A MOTHER

About the Author

Leslie Lehr Spirson, who grew up in Ohio, graduated with a B.A. from University of Southern California School of Cinema-Television. She also studied at Monterey Institute of International Studies and University of California-Los Angeles.

Her career has covered a broad spectrum of television, commercial and video, and film production. In television, she worked on "Fridays," "Doobie Brothers Farewell," and "David Frost's Guinness Book of Records." She has been production coordinator for Belinda Carlysle, the Fabulous Thunderbirds, Huey Lewis, and Z.Z. Top, as well as production manager for many national commercials.

She production coordinated feature films, including *Barfly*, *Prince: Sign of the Times*, and *Witchboard*.

She won a Governor's Bicentennial Award in 1976, as writer/producer/director of "Music of America," a video shown on WARL-TV in Columbus, Ohio, and an Emmy in 1982, as producer/production manager for "War Games," a video-drama, USC Cinema-Television.

She has written several original screenplays, and is co-producer of *Dibs*, a TV movie now in development, based on Dr. Virginia Axline's book, *Dibs: In Search of Self.*

She is currently working on a novel and another baby!

She and her husband and daughter live in Woodland Hills, California.

Suggested Reading

Axline, Virginia M. Dibs: *In Search of Self.* New York: Ballantine, 1964.

Brazelton, T. Berry. *What Every Baby Knows.* New York: Ballantine, 1988.

Eisenberg, Arlene, Heidi Eisenberg Markoff, and Sandee Eisenberg Hathaway. *What to Expect When You're Expecting.* New York: Workman, 1984.

White, Burton L. *The First Three Years of Life.* New York: Prentice-Hall, 1985.

Other Gift Books from CompCare Publishers

Falling in Fun Again, *Doris Jasinek and Pamela Bell Ryan*. A funfilled gift book, illustrated by Caroline Price, shows how to put the sparkle back into marriages, friendships, and other close encounters. 03939, 80pp, paperback

A Family Is a Circle of People Who Love You, *Doris Jasinek and Pamela Bell Ryan*. Two-color illustrations by Caroline Price brighten this celebration of families — including "families" made up of a patchwork of possibilities. 00372, 74pp, paperback

God Grant Me the Laughter, *Ed. F.* A collection of cartoons, quotes, and asides capture the relief and joy of recovery from alcoholism—and the camaraderie of AA. 03764, 200 pp, paperback

How to Build a House of Hearts, *Doris Jasinek and Pamela Bell Ryan.* This "heartbook, not a handbook, " with endearing drawings by Caroline Price, shows how to make everyone in the family feel worthy and loved. 03699, 64 pp, paperback

The Hug Therapy Book, *Kathleen Keating, drawings by Mimi Noland.* With a half-million in print and 15 foreign versions, this beloved little gift classic offers a new reason to hug — hug for health! 03251, 72 pp, paperback

Hug Therapy 2, *The Wonderful Language of Hugs, Kathleen Keating, drawings by Mimi Noland.* A treasure-house of more truths about hugs describes and demonstrates (with those charming bear illustrations) how hugs "speak" without speaking. 03632, 84pp, paperback

The Hug Therapy Book of Birthdays and Anniversaries, *messages and drawings by Mimi Noland.* This keepsake to record important days is based on Kathleen Keating's famous hug books. Includes a page per week and a place for addresses and phone numbers . 04127, 112pp, embossed hard cover

Perfect Parenting and Other Myths, *Frank Main, Ed. D.* Flawless Father and Magical Mother are myths from Someone Else's Family! A great book to help you shed unrealistic expectations and handle the complexities of parenting. 03392, 232 pp, paperback.

Stress Breakers, *Helene Lerner with Roberta Elins, cartoons by Peter Bastiensen.* Distills basics of stress reduction and relaxation and shows how to apply them in everyday living. A stress relief book that's actually fun! 03202, 110 pp, paperback

What's So Funny about Getting Old? *Ed Fischer and Jane Thomas Noland.* The perfect gift for anyone 50-plus, this book of cartoons, quips memory-joggers, and insights introduces a new comedy genre — "Elder humor." 04259, 128pp, paperback

Order Form

Order No.	Qty.	Title	Author	Unit Cost	Total
04333		Welcome to Club Mom	Lehr-Spirson, L.	$9.95	
03939		Falling in Fun Again	Jasinek/Ryan	$7.95	
00372		A Family is a Circle...	Jasinek/Ryan	$5.95	
03764		God Grant Me the Laughter	Ed F.	$7.95	
03699		How to Build a House of Hearts	Jasinek/Ryan	$5.95	
03251		Hug Therapy	Keating, K.	$5.95	
03632		Hug Therapy 2	Keating, K.	$5.95	
04127		Hug Therapy Birthday Book	Noland, M.	$12.95	
03392		Perfect Parenting and Other Myths	Main, F./Ed D.	$9.95	
03202		Stress Breakers	Lerner/Elins	$8.95	
04259		What's So Funny about Getting Old	Fischer/Noland	$6.95	

SHIPPING/HANDLING CHARGES

Amount of Order	Shipping Charges
$0-$10.00	$2.50
$10.01-$25.00	$3.50
$25.01-$50.00	$4.00
$50.01-$75.00	$5.00

Subtotal	
Shipping and Handling (see below)	
Add your state's sales tax	
TOTAL	

Send check or money order payable to CompCare Publishers. No cash or C.O.D.'s please. Quantity discounts available. Prices subject to change without notice.

Send book(s) to:

Name _____

Address _____

City _____ State _____ Zip _____

☐ Check enclosed for $_____, payable to CompCare Publishers

☐ Charge to my credit card   ☐ Visa   ☐ MasterCard   ☐ Discover

Account # _____ Exp. date _____

Signature_____Daytime Phone _____

CompCare® Publishers

2415 Annapolis Lane
Minneapolis, MN 55441
To order by phone call (612) 559-4800
or toll free (800) 328-3330